CELTIC REVISION NOTES – LAW

CRIMINAL LAW

CELTIC REVISION NOTES – LAW
General Advisor Editor John Marriage Q.C.

CRIMINAL LAW

by

D. Walker
LL.B (London) Cert.Ed. (Leeds)

CELTIC REVISION AIDS

CELTIC REVISION AIDS
Mayfield Road,
Walton-on-Thames Surrey, KT12 5PL

© C.E.S. Ltd.

First published 1981

ISBN 017 751 353 5

All rights reserved

Typeset by

Computacomp (UK) Ltd
Fort William, Scotland
Printed in Hong Kong

GENERAL EDITOR'S FOREWORD

To be asked to be consultant editor to this series and to provide a foreword is to me a great honour. I have never claimed to be the sort of lawyer who has anything to contribute to the academic sphere but I do I think know what is required for the administrator and executive in the ordinary world.

A series such as this can always be the subject of the gibe "a little learning is a dangerous thing" but I have seen enough of the commercial and administrative spheres to be certain that such a series is badly needed. In my student days there were two sorts of law book: the academic tome and the excellent "nut shell" which was designed to get the reader through the examination. Neither would ordinarily be of value to the embryo company secretary, accountant, banker or civil servant who ought to have a general grounding in the law in all its facets. I say "ought to" because I believe that in the absence of such a grounding the person concerned is inclined to become frightened of this, to him or her, mysterious discipline "the law". In its turn the practical result is that that person either sends every problem (and it is difficult to think of any commercial or administrative decision which does not have some legal problem within it) off to their Company's or Institution's already overworked legal department or solicitor. Worse still he or she may fail to see that there is a legal problem at all. When the latter happens, decisions can be taken on a completely false basis because the problem be it of contract, industrial relations, defamation or company law has not been detected. I often think that the role of the lawyer is to say "Wait! Has anyone considered the following problem ...?" I know this infuriates the non-lawyer but better the anger of colleagues at the decision-making stage than the receipt of a writ after the implementation of the decision.

GENERAL EDITOR'S FOREWORD

The aspect of Mr. Walker's books which I particularly like is his system of setting out the proposition and following that with a simple exposition of the facts and decision in a very few cases.

I also congratulate Mr. Walker on his economic selection of cases which not only illustrate the principles, but also takes the subject out of the recesses of the Law Library and into the real world.

To the reader I give the following advice: read these volumes as much as you need to pass your examination. Once qualified keep them by you for easy reference because however much the law may change (and it will) they will guide you to the existence of every day legal problems in your job, enable you to describe the problem to the lawyer and, most important of all, help you to understand what the lawyer is saying to you.

John Goodbody Marriage

One of Her Majesty's Counsel
A bencher of the Inner Temple
A Recorder.

CONTENTS

	page
AUTHOR'S FOREWORD	ix
CRIMINAL LAW	1

Definition of a crime – Constituents of a crime – Actus reus and mens rea – Attempts to commit a crime – Classification of offences – Necessity – Defences to criminal responsibility – (a) Infancy – (b) Mistake – (c) Drunkenness – (d) Insanity – (e) Diminished responsibility – (f) Provocation – (g) Justification

SPECIFIC OFFENCES 12

Murder – Manslaughter – Assault and battery– Infanticide – Child destruction – Concealment of birth – Abortion – Rape – Unlawful intercourse – Bigamy – Motoring offences – Theft – Robbery – Burglary –Obtaining by deception – Obtaining pecuniary advantage by deception – Blackmail – Handling stolen goods – Criminal damage – Miscellaneous – Offences against public order – Riot, Unlawful assembly, Rout – Affray – Treason – Sedition – Incitement to disaffection – Incitement to Mutiny Act 1797 – Official secrets – Firearms and offensive weapons – Obscene publications – Perjury

THE CRIMINAL PROCESS 38

Arrest – Judges' Rules 1964 – Bail Act 1976 – Punishments and other orders of a Criminal Court – Imprisonment – Suspended prison sentence – Hospital order – Borstal – Detention centres – Attendance centres – Care orders – Absolute discharge – Conditional discharge – Binding-over – Probation – Fine – Compensation order – Bankruptcy – Deferred sentence – Community Service Order

JURIES AND THE JUDICIARY 50

Composition of Juries – Challenging the Jury – Legal aid in criminal proceedings – **INDEX OF CASES** 57

CASES	61
PRACTICE QUESTIONS	114
WORKED EXAMPLES	116
GLOSSARY OF TERMS	127
EXAMINATION TECHNIQUE	129

AUTHOR'S FOREWORD

This book is intended for revision purposes and the materials have been collected with the Criminal Law syllabuses of the BEC National Diploma, RSA, certain professional examinations and G.C.E. "A" and "O" Level courses in mind. The contents will also prove useful for those students studying the BEC National Organisation and the Environment course.

The book should be studied in conjunction with a textbook in order to obtain a greater understanding of the subject as the sections contained herein are not intended to provide an exhaustive study of the subject but to explore those areas most frequently encountered in examination questions.

The Practice Questions included are not taken from specific papers, but are short questions aimed at testing the student's knowledge in areas which are essential to most examinations.

D. WALKER
Nottingham
March 1980

CRIMINAL LAW

DEFINITION OF A CRIME

A definition of crime is extremely difficult. In Halsbury's "Laws of England", it is defined as an unlawful act or default which is an offence against the public and renders the person guilty of the act liable to legal punishment.

Professor Kenny in his "Outlines of Criminal Law" states "Crimes are wrongs whose sanction is punitive and in no way remissible by any private person, but remissible by the Crown alone, if remissible at all".

Professor Glanville Williams' definition "A crime is a legal wrong that can be followed by criminal proceedings which may result in punishment" is a lawyer's definition and although apparently circulatory is worthy of consideration by the student.

CONSTITUENTS OF A CRIME

To secure a conviction the prosecution must normally prove **beyond all reasonable doubt** that the accused committed a guilty act or omission, or was found in a certain bodily position (R v Larsonneur) (**actus reus**) with guilty intent (**mens rea**), though in some modern statutory offences mens rea may no longer be a necessary element.

ACTUS REUS AND MENS REA

"Actus non facit reum, nisi mens sit rea" (an act is not unlawful unless the mind be guilty).

(a) **Actus Reus** may consist in an act or an omission (R v Gibbons and

Proctor 1918), depending on the definition of the crime charged. No person can be convicted unless his conduct falls within the definition of an established offence (R v Deller 1952; Ferguson v Weaving 1951).

(1) The Actus must be directly attributed to the accused. He is not liable for the actus of another person, unless he has incited such actus or shared a common purpose with the doer (contrast with vicarious liability in tort).

(2) The Actus must be the voluntary act of the accused, i.e. the product of his own free will. Coercion, automation, etc., are therefore valid defences.

(3) **Ignorantia juris haud excusat** – Ignorance of the law is no excuse.

(b) **Mens rea** – In Chisholm v Doulton (1889) Cave J. stated: "It is a general principle of our criminal law that there must be as an essential ingredient in a criminal offence some blameworthy condition of mind. Sometimes it is negligence, sometimes malice, sometimes guilty knowledge, but as a general rule there must be something of that kind which is designated by the expression mens rea."

There can be

(1) Intentional conduct, i.e. the consequences are foreseen and desired.
(2) Recklessness (gross negligence), i.e. the consequences are foreseen but not necessarily desired.
(3) Negligence, i.e. the consequences are not foreseen in circumstances where the law requires foresight.

It is interesting to note the remarks of Stephen J. in the case of R v Tolson (1889) on the maxim "non est reus, nisi mens sit rea".

"Though this phrase is in common use, I think it most unfortunate, and not only likely to mislead, but actually misleading on the following grounds. It naturally suggests that, apart from all particular definitions of crimes, such a thing exists as "mens rea" or "guilty mind", which is always expressly or by implication involved in every definition. This is obviously not the case, for the mental elements of different crimes differ widely. 'Mens rea' means in the case of murder, malice aforethought; in the case of theft, an intention to steal; in the case of rape, an intention to have forcible connection with a woman without her consent; and in the case of receiving stolen goods, knowledge that the goods were stolen. In some cases it denotes mere inattention. For instance, in the case of manslaughter by negligence it may mean forgetting to notice a signal. It appears confusing to call so many dissimilar states of mind by one name. It seems contradictory indeed to describe a mere absence of mind as a 'mens rea' or guilty mind."

Some modern statutes impose absolute liability (no mens rea required) and once the actus reus has been proved against the accused, he must be convicted whatever his state of mind at the time. A case of notoriety is R v Larsonneur (1933). However, in Sweet v Parsley (1969), the House of Lords approved the following statement of the High Court of Australia in Proudman v Dayman (1941) "As a general rule an honest and reasonable belief in a state of facts which if they existed, would make the defendant's act innocent affords an excuse for doing what would otherwise be an offence." The House of Lords held that mens rea as an essential ingredient could only be excluded by express words or necessary implication in the Act of Parliament creating the offence.

Strict liability occurs in matters concerning road traffic, food, drink and tobacco. Justification for liability in such cases was discussed by Lord Reid in Warner v Metropolitan Police Commissioner (1968). "These are only quasi-criminal offences and it does not really offend the ordinary man's sense of justice that moral guilt is not of the essence of the offence."

Dean Roscoe Pound also justified strict liability by saying: "Such statutes are not meant to punish the vicious will but to put pressure upon the thoughtless and inefficient to do their whole duty in the interest of public health or safety or morals."

ATTEMPTS TO COMMIT A CRIME

The Criminal Law seeks to punish the incompetent offender as well as the successful criminal. A person may be convicted of an attempt if he embarks on a series of acts which if not interrupted would result in the actual commission of a crime. **Example:** Soaking a building with petrol in order to commit arson.

The questions to be decided by the jury are
(1) Were the acts of the accused consistent with an intent to commit a crime?
(2) How close did the accused come to a completed offence?

There must be an overt act sufficiently proximate to the intended crime (Davey v Lee 1968).

Although attempt implies the intent, an intent will not necessarily imply an attempt. The attempt must be evidenced by an overt act forming part of a series of acts which, if not interrupted would result in the commission of the actual offence (R v Linneker 1906).

Neither can a reckless state of mind be sufficient mens rea for an attempt (R v Mohan 1975).

The impossibility of performance of the act intended does not of itself render the attempt guiltless, for example, an attempt to pick an empty pocket (R v Ring 1892), but see Haughton v Smith (1973) where an attempt to commit a substantive offence was impossible. The accused will however be guilty of an offence if it is merely the method used which results in the attempt being impossible of fulfilment, for example, a burglar whose house-breaking implements are inadequate for the job, the potential assassin who fires at his victim who is out of range and the potential poisoner who administers an inadequate dose. Mere preparatory work (R v Easin 1971) is not sufficient for an attempt, but if a course of action is thwarted (R v Button 1900) conviction for an attempt is possible.

It is possible to attempt to commit an offence of strict liability, but the attempt requires mens rea, even though the completed offence does not (Gardner v Akeroyd 1952).

CLASSIFICATION OF OFFENCES

(a) **Indictable Offences** – These are serious offences triable by a judge and jury for which a Bill of Indictment sets out the charges against the accused in the Crown Court. The indictment gives the accused notice of the charge against him and if he is not proved to have committed the offence charged, he must be acquitted even though clearly guilty of a different offence (Partridge v Crittenden). Examples of indictable offences are murder, treason, robbery, and causing death by dangerous driving.

(b) **Summary Offences** – The word summary refers to the method of procedure, there being no jury on summary trial. Formerly such offences were known as petty offences, but this term was not considered serious enough for breaches of the law. Cases which fall under this heading are those which are expressed by statute to be punishable only on summary convictions and include most offences under the Road Traffic Act 1972; being drunk and disorderly (Licensing Act 1872); being a suspected person (Vagrancy Act 1824 s.4) as amended by Criminal Law Act 1967 Schedule 2. Also offences falling within Schedule 1 of the Criminal Law Act 1977, such as assault on the police, driving whilst unfit through drink or drugs or with blood alcohol level over the prescribed limit. Other examples of summary offences are, flying a kite near an airfield, "feeding" a parking meter, a driver failing to sign his driving licence, talking to a bus driver whilst the bus is in motion, listening to fire brigade or pirate radio stations on the radio.

(c) **Hybrid Offences** – In these cases, if the magistrates decide the case is fit for summary trial they will try the case provided the defendant agrees to be tried by them rather than by a judge and jury at the Crown Court. Examples are theft, obtaining property or a pecuniary advantage by deception, taking vehicles, burglary not involving violence, malicious wounding, assault occasioning actual bodily harm, gross indecency between men, unlawful sexual intercourse with a girl over 13 but under 16.

Some offences are made triable either way by the statute creating them, for example, living on the earnings of prostitution (Sexual Offences Act 1956 s.30); importuning by a man (Sexual Offences Act 1956 s.32); possession of a controlled drug (Misuse of Drugs Act 1971 s.5(2)); reckless driving (R.T.A. 1972 s.2).

Some offences are triable either way depending on the value of the property, for example, offences other than arson under Section 1 of the Criminal Damage Act 1971 where the value of the property involved is less than £200.

(d) **Arrestable Offences** – An arrestable offence is defined by the Criminal Law Act 1967 as one for which the sentence is fixed by law, e.g. murder, or for which a person (not previously convicted) may be sentenced to a term of imprisonment for at least five years. At common law any person, whether a constable or not may arrest anyone committing an "arrestable offence" in his presence, or whom he reasonably suspects to be in the act of committing such an offence.

Non-arrestable offences are not defined by the Act, but include all other offences.

NECESSITY

An act or omission which amounts to a crime cannot normally be justified by necessity, for a particular act is never necessary in the sense that there is no alternative. Even if the only alternative is death, this does not justify a crime. See R v Dudley and Stephens (1884) and Buckoke v Greater London Council (1971).

If we accept Professor Glanville Williams' definition of necessity as "a law being broken to achieve a greater good" it becomes apparent that even if necessity is not a defence, it may make conduct excusable; note the light sentence in R v Dudley and Stephens. Indeed some statutes recognise necessity within the definition of particular offences.

(1) Protection of Animals Act 1911 penalises the infliction of "unnecessary suffering".
(2) Road Traffic Act 1974 provides that vehicles may be parked on verges and footways if this is necessary to save life or for other similar purposes.

The decisions in R v Bourne (1938) and Leigh v Gladstone (1909) were based on necessity although the former case was superseded by the Abortion Act and in the latter only assault and battery as a tort was considered.

The position of necessity in respect of driving offences indicated in Buckoke v G.L.C. was that necessity could not justify the driver of a fire engine crossing against the lights in order to save life. Whilst rejecting the defence however, Lord Denning indicated that the solution to the problem was a generous exercise of discretion in deciding whether or not to prosecute.

The only case in which necessity was recognised was in Johnson v Phillips (1976) but here the doctrine was used to support a conviction. The law's attitude is therefore best illustrated by the story of the Manchester G.P. who passed a police car that had flagged him down for speeding and in order to show the urgency of his mission he waved his stethoscope at the police officials. The police car rapidly overtook him, one of the policeman waving a pair of handcuffs to illustrate the urgency of their mission.

DEFENCES TO CRIMINAL RESPONSIBILITY

(a) Infancy

The law presumes children under ten are doli incapax (incapable of committing a crime) so in Walters v Luns (1951) the parents could not be guilty of receiving stolen goods when they acquired a tricycle taken by their seven-year old son. Since the 1968 Theft Act the parents would be guilty of theft since their actions amounted to an appropriation.

Between the ages of ten and 14 a child is liable for any crime he commits if the prosecution proves that the child knew that what he was doing was wrong.

There is an irrebuttable presumption that a boy under 14 cannot be convicted of rape although he can be prosecuted for the lesser offence of indecent assault.

A person over the age of 14, in statutory language, a young person, is liable for criminal acts, but if under the age of 17 is usually tried in Juvenile Court.

No person under the age of 17 can be sent to prison. An offender who has attained 17 but who is under 21 may not be sent to prison unless the court, having obtained information about the circumstances of the offence and considered his character and physical and mental condition is of the opinion that no other method of dealing with him is appropriate. In such a case the court has to decide whether he should serve a short sentence of up to six months or a long term sentence of at least three years. It cannot impose a sentence (or sentences) which involve a term of more than six months and less than three years.

(b) Mistake

Mistake as to the law is never an excuse for a criminal act. The rule is ignorantia haud excusat (Ignorance of the law is no excuse). The only exception to this is where an Act of Parliament or Statutory Instrument containing that particular law has not been published at the time of the alleged offence.

Mistake of fact will be a defence if it is reasonable and if the facts were as believed, no offence would have been committed (R v Levett 1638; R v Hibbert 1869), but the mistake must relate to some fact essential to the charge (R v Prince 1875) although the distinction of this case from the facts of R v Hibbert is very fine.

Criminal liability will not of course be excluded through ignorance of the law; See R v Bailey (1800).

A man cannot be convicted of rape if he believed, albeit mistakenly, that the woman gave her consent even though he had no reasonable grounds for that belief – D.P.P. v Morgan and see Sexual Offences (Amendment) Act 1976.

The question is whether the belief is honestly held, not whether it is reasonable. The test is subjective in relation to circumstances.

(c) Drunkenness

Although the consumption of alcohol is not generally an offence, there are certain offences of drunkenness amongst the more important of which are:

(1) Being found drunk in a public place.
(2) Being drunk and disorderly in a public place.
(3) Being drunk in a public place in possession of a loaded firearm.
(4) Being found drunk in a public place in charge of a child under seven years of age.
(5) Being under the influence of drink or drugs when in charge of a motor-vehicle.
(6) Having a blood-alcohol concentration above 80 milligrams of alcohol in 100 millilitres of blood when in charge of a motor vehicle.

To combat acute cases of alcoholism, the Home Secretary is empowered under the Criminal Justice Act 1972 to set up medical treatment centres for alcoholics against whom a criminal charge would otherwise have been preferred.

Drunkenness is however only a defence to a crime if it prevents the formation of mens rea, such as in dishonesty in theft. It is not a defence to abnormally violent behaviour (R v Majewski 1976). Indeed, the Butler Committee on Mentally Abnormal Offenders proposed that there should be a new offence of dangerous voluntary intoxication. Since Majewski's case it appears that drunkenness can negative mens rea in crimes of specific intent such as murder, but not in crimes of basic intent such as assault.

If a person gets drunk in order to commit a crime, his prior mens rea may be coupled with a later act (A.G. for Northern Ireland v Gallagher 1963).

It is no defence that drunkenness makes a person more ready to commit a crime. See D.P.P. v Beard (1920), R v Howell (1974), R v Sheehan and Moore (1975).

Similar rules apply to the taking of drugs and their effect on criminal responsibility.

(d) Insanity

As a defence is governed by the principles laid down in McNaghten's Case (1843)

(1) Every man is presumed sane until the contrary is proved. The onus of proof lies with the defence and is on a balance of probabilities.

(2) To establish a defence on the ground of insanity it must be clearly proved that, at the time of committing the act, the party accused was labouring under such a defect of reason, from disease of the mind, as not to know the nature and quality of the act he was doing, or if he did know it, that he did not know he was doing what was wrong.

By the Criminal Procedure (Insanity) Act 1964 the verdict in such cases is "Not guilty by reason of insanity" and the defendant will be detained indefinitely in hospital which may be worse than a prison sentence and since the abolition of capital punishment it may be observed that the accused would have to be mad to rely on this defence.

A malfunctioning of the mind of transitory effect caused by the application to the body of some external factor is not a "disease of the mind" within the meaning of the McNaghten Rules. Such malfunctioning, if self-induced or induced by a failure to take appropriate precautions will not relieve an accused person from criminal responsibility but in other cases it may entitle him to an acquittal (R v Quick 1973; R v Paddison 1973).

"Wrong" in the McNaghten Rules means contrary to law. Where it is shown that the accused knew that what he was doing was contrary to law the trial judge may withdraw the issue of insanity from the jury (R v Windle 1952).

The defence of automatism is based on an abnormal state of consciousness, e.g. confusion, delusion or disassociation that is regarded as incompatible with the existence of mens rea, but does not amount to insanity. Automatism was defined in Bratty v Attorney-General for Northern Ireland (1963).

"No act is punishable if it is done involuntarily and an involuntary act in this context — some people nowadays prefer to speak of it as automatism — means an act done by the muscles without any control by the mind such as a spasm, a reflex action or a convulsion or an act done by a person who is not conscious of what he is doing, such as an act done while suffering from concussion, or while sleepwalking."

The main areas of automatism are
(1) Sleepwalking (This defence has been accepted in the case of a driver who got up in the middle of the night and had a motor-cycle accident).
(2) Concussion.
(3) Epilepsy.
(4) Hypoglycaemia (deficiency of blood-sugar); See R v Quick (1973).
(5) Dissociative states (hysterical neurosis — split-personality or a severe psychological blow such as rejection by a lover) — See Hill v Baxter (1958), R v Charlson (1955) and R v Kemp 1956).

(e) Diminished responsibility

Introduced by the Homicide Act of 1957 Section 2 which states "Where a person kills or is a party to the killing of another he shall not be convicted of murder if he was suffering from such abnormality of mind (whether arising from a condition of arrested or retarded development of mind or any inherent causes or induced by disease or injury) as substantially impaired his mental responsibility for his acts or omissions in doing or being a party to the killing."

Abnormality of mind was defined in R v Byrne (1960) by Parker C.J. as: "a state of mind so different from that of ordinary human beings that the reasonable man would term it abnormal. It appears to us to be wide enough to cover the mind's activities in all its aspects."

The prosecution can reply with evidence of insanity.

A successful defence results in acquittal on a charge of murder but a conviction on a charge of manslaughter often resulting in life imprisonment and in effect negativing the defence although a hospital order was laid down as a general principle in R v Morris (1961) where punishment as such is not intended.

(f) Provocation

Is only a defence insofar as it reduces a charge of murder to manslaughter. Provocation was defined in R v Duffy (1949) as "some act or series of acts, done by the dead man to the accused which would cause in any reasonable person, and actually causes in the accused, a sudden and temporary loss of self-control, rendering the accused so subject to passion as to make him or her for the moment not master of his mind."

(g) Justification

Usually involved in self-defence. A person is entitled to use reasonable force in defence of himself or of others or in defence of his property (R v Hussey 1924). Although this decision has been criticised it still remains a good precedent.

SPECIFIC OFFENCES

MURDER

The legal term for killing a man, whether lawfully or unlawfully is "homicide".

Examples of lawful homicide are self-defence and the execution of a person sentenced to death by a competent court.

Common law examples of unlawful homicide are murder and manslaughter. Statutory examples include suicide pacts, infanticide and causing death by dangerous driving.

Chief Justice Coke's classic definition of murder is "Unlawfully killing a reasonable creature in being and under the Queen's peace with malice aforethought either expressed by the party or implied by law, the death following within a year and a day."

"Unlawfully" means without justification or excuse.

"Reasonable creature" means a human being.

"In being" implies an existence independent from the mother.

"Malice aforethought" describes the mens rea of murder and as a Royal Commission on Capital Punishment commented, is simply a comprehensive name for a number of different mental attitudes. The words do not imply any special ill-will or careful preparation beforehand and the mens rea may merely be a flash of temper.

Death following within a year and a day, see R v Dyson (1908).

Usually the mens rea is either
(1) an intent to kill or
(2) an intent to inflict grievous bodily harm (D.P.P. v Smith 1961), or
(3) risk taking of a certain kind (Hyman v D.P.P. 1974).

If at the time of death an original wound is still a substantial and an operating cause, the death may be held to be the result of that wound, even though some other cause of death was operating. See R v Smith (1959) but see also R v Jordan (1956).

The fact that, because of religious convictions a victim of wounding declines a blood transfusion which would have saved his life does not act as a break in the causal connection between the act of wounding and death (R v Blaue 1975).

Intent to murder can be transferred (R v Gore 1613).

On conviction, the punishment for murder is life imprisonment. The Home Secretary has power to release a prisoner on licence, he is however subject to recall, and may be sent back to prison at any time. Usually a licence is only revoked if the prisoner does not co-operate with his supervising officer, wilfully fails to keep in regular employment or associates with known criminals.

Each prison has a local review committee, (usually the governor, a magistrate, and a probation officer) which considers release on licence at first instance. This committee reports to the Parole Board (which must include a judge, a psychiatrist, a person experienced in the after-care of prisoners and a criminologist) which makes the final recommendation to the Home Secretary.

MANSLAUGHTER

There are two broad classes, voluntary and involuntary, each attracting a maximum sentence of life imprisonment.

(1) Voluntary manslaughter

Although there is malice aforethought present, the crime is manslaughter and not murder, if the accused establishes diminished responsibility or the prosecution fails to disprove a plea of provocation, suicide pact or infanticide (supra).

Homicide Act 1957, Sections 3 and 4
Section 3

Where on a charge of murder there is evidence on which the jury can find that the person charged has provoked (whether by things done or by things said or both together) to lose his self-control, the question whether the provocation was enough to make a reasonable man do as he did shall be left to be determined by the jury; and in determining that question the jury shall take into account everything both done and said according to the effect which, in their opinion, it would have on a reasonable man. R v Duffy (1949); R v Byrne (1960); R v Davies (1975); Mancini v D.P.P. (1942); R v Brown (1972); Edwards v R (1973).

Section 4 (1)

It shall be manslaughter, and shall not be murder, for a person acting in pursuance of a suicide pact between him and another to kill the other or be a party to the other killing himself or being killed by a third person.

Section 4(2)

Where it is shown that a person charged with the murder of another killed the other or was a party to his killing himself or being killed, it shall be for the defence to prove that the person charged was acting in pursuance of a suicide pact between him and the other.

Section 4(3)

For the purposes of this section "suicide pact" means a common agreement between two or more persons having for its object the death of all of them, whether or not each is to take his own life, but nothing done by a person who enters into a suicide pact shall be treated as done by him in pursuance of the pact unless it is done while he has the settled intention of dying in pursuance of the pact.

The requirements of the Suicide Act 1961 should however be noted:

The Suicide Act 1961

1   The rule of law whereby it is a crime for a person to commit suicide is hereby abrogated.
2(1)   A person who aids, abets, counsels, or procures the suicide of another, or an attempt by another to commit suicide shall be liable on conviction on indictment to imprisonment for a term not exceeding fourteen years.

(2) Involuntary manslaughter

Is committed where death results from an act not intended to kill or cause grievous bodily harm but nevertheless intended to do some lesser harm. See D.P.P. v Newbury (1976).

Also includes manslaughter by omission for in spite of the injunction of The New Decalogue,

"Thou shalt not kill: but need'st not strive officiously to keep alive," there are certain instances where breach of a duty leading to death will

result in a conviction for manslaughter. The principle instances at common law are:
(1) The duty of parents (or those in loco parentis) in respect of children.
(2) Duties arising between cohabiting spouses.
(3) The duty arising from the custody of helpless persons.
(4) Duties arising in some cases from having given an undertaking to take safety precautions (e.g. railway crossing keepers).

Constructive manslaughter means killing in the course of certain kinds of unlawful acts where the defendant is negligent as to causing bodily injury (R v Church).

Constructive manslaughter requires that the defendant:
(1) Should have committed an intentional or reckless offence against the person.
(2) Should have been at least negligent as to causing some injury in consequence.

ASSAULT AND BATTERY

These terms are frequently confused as even in the courts they are used carelessly and the statutory expressions "common assault" and "indecent assault" actually refer to battery.

An assault is in fact an intentional or reckless act which creates in the mind of another a fear of imminent batter. Two things must be considered.
(1) The victim must expect that force is about to be applied to him. He need not experience fear, but he must expect to be hit.
(2) The accused must intend to create the expectation or be reckless as to it. In other words, it is sufficient that he knows he is doing something from which the belief is likely to arise. Fagan v Metropolitan Police Commissioner (1969).

It must of course be possible for force to be applied, therefore shaking a fist at someone across a river is not an assault, but an assault can be committed from the other side of a locked door if the victim believes the attacker is about to break it down. In an old case (Smith v Newsum 1674) a woman, standing in a cutler's shop was held liable for assault when she shook a sword at the plaintiff who was at the other side of the street.

It is an assault to point a gun at someone, even if it is unloaded, for the victim will be placed in fear.

Words in themselves cannot constitute an assault (Turberville v Savage 1669), but words accompanied by some other conduct may be sufficient to constitute an assault (Read v Coker 1853).

It is a defence to prove that the assault or battery was accidental, e.g. jostling in a crowd, provided the action was unintentional. Even if the assault was deliberate, e.g. splashing with water, Section 44 of the Offences against the Person Act 1861 gives magistrates the power to draw up a certificate of dismissal if the assault was so trifling as not to merit punishment. Such certificates will bar a civil action in respect of the same offence. Coward v Baddeley (1859).

Assault can be transferred as where a person throws a stone intending to hit one person and hits another by mistake.

Consent to an assault is no defence (R v Donovan 1934).

For common assault or battery the maximum punishment is one year's imprisonment.

The Offences Against the Person Act 1861 creates specific offences where the battery is more serious. Section 18 as amended by the Criminal Law Act 1967 states,

"Whosoever shall unlawfully and maliciously wound or cause any grievous bodily harm to any person, with intent to do some grievous bodily harm to any person, or with intent to resist or prevent the lawful apprehension of any person, shall be punishable with imprisonment for life."

Usually this section is referred to as creating the crime of "wounding with intent".

Section 20 of the Act states:

"Whosoever shall unlawfully and maliciously wound or inflict any grievous bodily harm upon any other person either with or without any weapon, or instrument shall be guilty of a misdemeanour."

A person may be guilty of unlawfully and maliciously inflicting grievous bodily harm even though he was acting out of mere mischief (R v Martin 1881).

Also if a man creates in another's mind an immediate sense of danger which causes such a person to try to escape, and in doing so he injures himself, the person who creates such a state of mind is responsible for the injuries which result. R v Halliday (1889).

Section 47 of the Act states:

"Whosoever shall be convicted upon an indictment of any assault occasioning actual bodily harm shall be liable to be kept in penal servitude and whosoever shall be convicted upon an indictment for a common assault shall be liable at the discretion of the Court, to be imprisoned for any term not exceeding one year with or without hard labour."

The punishments mentioned are no longer effective but it can be seen that Section 47 is almost in accordance with Section 20 and being a lesser offence a person charged under Section 20 could be convicted under Section 47. Neither Section 20 nor 47 can be used in substitution for Section 18 as this section does not require an assault. Section 20 has been held to include assault by virtue of the word "inflicts".

INFANTICIDE

Where a woman wilfully causes the death of her child under the age of twelve months, but the balance of her mind is disturbed by the birth or lactation, she is guilty of infanticide and not of murder. (Infanticide Act 1938.) The offence is punishable in the same way as manslaughter although usually a probation order or a discharge is given. Since the introduction of Diminished Responsibility the offence is not necessary although it is useful in sparing a woman the distress of being charged with murder.

The Act does not apply to lesser offences such as attempted murder or unlawful wounding, nor is it a defence to the killing of a husband or another child although as the defence is based on a disturbed mind it would seem logical to extend it to all cases.

CHILD DESTRUCTION

This offence is committed by destroying the life of an unborn child before it has an existence separate from its mother. (Infant Life (Preservation) Act 1929.) The Act provides a presumption that a child is capable of being born alive after the 28th week of pregnancy.

CONCEALMENT OF BIRTH

It is an offence, punishable by two year's imprisonment, to secretly dispose of the dead body of a child to endeavour to conceal its birth and this is whether the child died before, at, or after birth.

ABORTION

Is an offence under the Offences Against the Person Act 1861 Section 58.

"Every woman being with child who, with intent to procure her own miscarriage, shall unlawfully administer to herself any poison or other noxious thing or shall unlawfully use any instrument or other means whatsoever with the like intent, and whosoever, with intent to procure the miscarriage of any woman, whether she be or be not with child, shall unlawfully administer to her or cause to be taken by her any poison or other noxious thing, or shall use any instrument or other means whatsoever with the like intent shall be liable to imprisonment for life." See R v Bourne (1939) now superseded by The Abortion Act 1967, which provides:

(1) Subject to the provisions of this section, a person shall not be guilty of an offence under the law relating to abortion when a pregnancy is terminated by a registered medical practitioner if two registered medical practitioners are of the opinion, formed in good faith
 (a) that the continuance of the pregnancy would involve risk to the life of the pregnant woman, or of injury to the physical or mental health of the pregnant woman or any existing children of her family, greater than if the pregnancy were terminated; or
 (b) that there is a substantial risk that if the child were born it would suffer from such physical or mental abnormalities as to be seriously handicapped.
(2) In determining whether the continuance of the pregnancy would involve such risk of injury to health as is mentioned in paragraph (a) of subsection (1) of this section, account may be taken of the pregnant woman's actual or reasonably foreseeable environment.
(3) Except as provided by subsection (4) of this section, any treatment for the termination of pregnancy must be carried out in a hospital vested in the Minister of Health or the Secretary of State under the National Health Service Acts, or in a place for the time being

approved for the purposes of this section by the said Minister or the Secretary of State.
(4) Subsection (3) of this section, and so much of subsection (1) as relates to the opinion of two registered medical practitioners, shall not apply to the termination of a pregnancy by a registered medical practitioner in a case where he is of the opinion, formed in good faith, that the termination is immediately necessary to save the life or to prevent grave permanent injury to the physical or mental health of the pregnant woman.

RAPE

Although an offence from the dawn of time, rape was not given a statutory definition until the Sexual Offences (Amendment) Act 1976, which placed the decision in R v Morgan on a statutory basis.

Section 1(1) provides: A man commits rape if
(a) he has unlawful sexual intercourse with a woman who at the time of the intercourse does not consent to it and
(b) at that time he knows that she does not consent to the intercourse or he is reckless as to whether she consents to it.

As a general rule a husband cannot be guilty of rape on his wife, although this rule does not apply in circumstances in which the wife's assent to marital intercourse may be considered as having been revoked, as in the case of judicial separation. A husband has no right, however, to use force or violence in order to exercise his right to intercourse. R v Miller (1954). His right to intercourse stops however on the issue of an injunction by the court or the husband has given an undertaking to avoid the issue of an injunction.

As the essence of rape is unlawful sexual intercourse with a woman without her consent by force, fear or fraud, if intercourse is obtained by persuading a woman that what was being done to her was not an act of sexual intercourse, it is rape, even though the woman may have given her consent to what was being done to her (R v Williams 1923). A decree nisi terminates a marriage for purposes of rape. R v O'Brien (1974).

A boy of under 14 is presumed incapable of rape which is rather illogical as the essence of the crime is merely penetration. A boy of under 14 who commits what is essentially rape can however be convicted of indecent assault.

The burden of proof as to the absence of the woman's consent rests with the prosecution.

UNLAWFUL INTERCOURSE

Neither the girl's consent nor the accused's mistake concerning her age is a defence to a charge of unlawful intercourse, but there are two statutory defences which may be available against a charge of unlawful intercourse with a girl who is under the age of sixteen.

(1) If a man has gone through a form of marriage with such a girl, it is a defence for him to prove that he had reasonable cause to believe that the girl was his wife.

(2) Section 6(3) of the Sexual Offences Act provides "A man is not guilty of an offence under this section because he has unlawful sexual intercourse with a girl under the age of 16, if he is under the age of 24 and has not previously been charged with a like offence and he believes her to be of the age of 16 or over and has reasonable cause for that belief."

This defence does not however apply in respect of a charge of intercourse with a girl under 13.

Neither does the defence apply in respect of a charge of indecent assault.

It appears to be of no account that the defendant has a list of convictions for indecent assault, rape or even for sexual intercourse with a girl under 13. No evidence can be given of any of these matters so that he will still be regarded as of unblemished character for the purpose of raising a defence under Section 6.

The burden of proof in respect of statutory exceptions is placed on the defendant but he need only establish the defence on the balance of probability.

A parent and any person who has "custody" or "care" of a young girl under 16 is guilty of an offence if he or she causes or encourages an indecent assault on the girl and a person who fails to prevent an offence, encourages it in law.

By Section 25 of the Sexual Offences Act 1956 the owner, occupier or manager of premises on which sexual offences take place is guilty of an offence if he knowingly suffers it and this covers a parent who allows a son or daughter to misbehave at home. A prosecution can also be maintained under Section 33 of the Sexual Offences Act which provides that it is an offence to allow promiscuity on premises, even by adults and even though no payment is made.

Indecent assault

An indecent assault is an assault accompanied by indecency. No definition of the term exists, but it has been held that kissing a girl against her will with a suggestion of sexual activity will suffice (R v Leeson 1968). Consent negatives an indecent assault as it does a common assault unless of course the assault is such as to cause an unlawful degree of bodily harm, or if the person assaulted is under 16.

It is essential that the accused should have been guilty of an assault: an invitation to perform indecent acts is not an indecent assault unless accompanied by force or the threat of force, (Fairclough v Whipp 1951) or even a slight touch (Beal v Kelly 1951).

By the Sexual Offences Act Section 14 and Schedule 2 as amended an indecent assault by any person (man or woman) on a woman is a dual offence punishable with two years imprisonment (five years if the offence is committed against a girl under 13).

In contrast Section 15 which applies to an indecent assault by any person (man or woman) on a man lays down a maximum of ten year's imprisonment.

Sexual Offences (Amendment) Act 1976

1. For the purposes of Section 1 of the Sexual Offences Act 1956 a man commits rape if
   (a) he has unlawful sexual intercourse with a woman who at the time of the intercourse does not consent to it; and
   (b) at that time he knows that she does not consent to the intercourse or is reckless as to whether she consents to it;
   and references to rape in other enactments (including the following provisions of this Act) shall be construed accordingly.
2. It is hereby declared that if at a trial for a rape offence the jury has to consider whether a man believed that a woman was consenting to sexual intercourse, the presence or absence of reasonable grounds for such a belief is a matter to which the jury is to have regard, in conjunction with any other relevant matters, in considering whether he so believed.

BIGAMY

By the Offences against the Person Act 1861 Section 57, bigamy is committed when "Whoever being married, goes through a ceremony of marriage with any other person during the life of his or her spouse is guilty of bigamy."

The punishment for bigamy is a maximum of seven years imprisonment.

The essential features of bigamy are
  (1) The existence of a valid marriage.
  (2) Its subsistence at the time of a second ceremony.
  (3) The second ceremony.

In addition
  (1) The first marriage must have been valid (R v Willshire 1861).
  (2) It is a defence that the accused believed on reasonable grounds that his or her spouse was dead although there has not been the absence for seven years necessary to support presumption of death.
  (3) It is a defence that the first marriage was void.
  (4) It is a defence that the first marriage has been dissolved.
  (5) If the other party to a bigamous marriage knows of the subsistence of the first marriage he or she will be guilty of aiding and abetting the crime of bigamy.

Bigamy is frowned upon by the law for a variety of reasons. It upsets the social order. It undermines the sanctity of the marriage ceremony and it may be a weapon of seduction, i.e. if a convicted man has seduced the innocent party before going through the marriage ceremony he may be rewarded with a lesser sentence, since it is assumed that the lady concerned has suffered correspondingly less as a result of the fraudulent ceremony.

MOTORING OFFENCES

Inconsiderate Driving – This is an offence under Section 3 of the Road Traffic Act 1972 as amended although charges under this section are infrequent. The offence is driving without reasonable consideration for other persons using the road and includes such things as:

(1) Stopping and starting a motor car and proceeding very slowly to annoy a following driver.
(2) Driving too slowly with malicious intent.
(3) Driving in a slow procession to make a demonstration.
(4) Queue-jumping.
(5) Splashing pedestrians.

Careless driving – This is the other offence created by Section 3 and is committed if a driver fails to attain the standard of care and attention; it refers to property as well as person and is an objective standard applying both to expert and to learner-driver. It may be careless driving to drive a motor-vehicle which is unroadworthy although in such a case it is more probable that a charge will be made under the Motor Vehicle (Construction and Use) Regulations 1973 which take effect not only against the person driving but also against the owner of the vehicle.

The penalty for careless and inconsiderate driving is a fine of up to £500.

Reckless driving – There is no definition of reckless driving but it is taken by the courts to mean knowingly taking risks in driving. The offence can be tried summarily or upon indictment and in the latter case is imprisonable up to two years.

Causing death by reckless driving is an offence triable only on indictment. On conviction disqualification from driving is obligatory in the absence of special reasons. The maximum sentence is five years imprisonment although it is rare that a sentence of over two years is imposed, and in most cases a fine and disqualification is imposed.

If the jury are not satisfied that the reckless driving caused the death they can convict of reckless driving simpliciter.

Driving under the influence of drink or drugs – Under Section 5 of the 1972 Act a person is guilty of an offence where he drives or attempts to drive, or is in charge of a motor-vehicle on a road or other public place when unfit to drive through drink or drugs.

Section 6 renders it an offence if a person drives or attempts to drive, or is in charge of a motor-vehicle on a road or other public place, having consumed alcohol in such quantity that the proportion in his blood, as ascertained by a laboratory test of blood or urine, exceeds the prescribed limit (80mg of alcohol per 100ml of blood, or 107mg of alcohol per 100ml of urine).

Both offences are summary although punishable with up to six months imprisonment.

Disqualification is discretionary, but a person who drives or attempts to drive when unfit or with the forbidden quantity of alcohol in his system, having been convicted of such an offence within the previous ten years is subject to a compulsory disqualification for three years in the absence of special reasons.

Virtually all traffic offences are construed to carry strict liability unless they require fault, hence a driver may be guilty of exceeding the speed limit even though the sign is obscured, or even on the most carefully maintained car the brakes may fail plunging the driver into criminal liability.

THEFT

Section 1 Theft Act 1968 provides that:

"A person is guilty of theft if he dishonestly appropriates property belonging to another with the intention of permanently depriving the other of it, and 'thief' and 'steal' shall be construed accordingly."

The Actus reus is therefore the appropriation of property belonging to another whilst the mens rea is the intention of doing so dishonestly and intending to permanently deprive the owner.

Dishonestly is not defined by Section 1, but as the offence involves serious moral stigma, there must be proof of a guilty mind.

Section 2 of the Act provides that a person will not be acting dishonestly while fulfilling one of the following conditions:

(1) He believes that he has a right to do so – Sam's friend owes him £5 so Sam takes the money from his friend's wallet.
(2) He believes the other would consent – Sam whilst visiting his friend helps himself to a glass of sherry.
(3) He believes the owner cannot be found – Sam finds a five pound note on the pavement.

Appropriation usually means taking. Section 3 provides

"Any assumption by a person of the right of an owner amounts to an appropriation and this includes where he has come by the property (innocently or not) without stealing it any later assumption of a right to it by keeping or dealing with it as owner." (See R v Eason and Lawrence v Metropolitan Police Commissioner).

Property is defined by Section 4 of the Theft Act and includes money and all other property, real or personal including things in action and other intangible property. Some items have a rather peculiar status with regard to theft, however, for Section 4 also provides:

"A person who picks mushrooms growing wild on any land, or who picks flowers, fruit or foliage from a plant growing wild on any land does not (although not in possession of the land) steal what he picks, unless he does it for reward or for sale or other commercial purpose."

Belonging to another is clarified by Section 5 of the Act which provides:

"Property shall be regarded as belonging to any person having possession or control of it, or having in it any proprietary right or interest (not being an equitable interest arising only from an agreement to transfer or grant an interest)."

Thus a co-owner or partner may steal property of which he is a co-owner or in which he has a partnership interest. A person may also be guilty of stealing his own property as in R v Turner (1971) where the defendant removed the car from a garage without permission and without paying for repairs.

With the intention of permanently depriving; Section 6 provides:

"A person appropriating property belonging to another without meaning the other to lose the thing itself is nevertheless to be regarded as having the intention of permanently depriving the other of it if his intention is to treat the thing as his own to dispose of regardless of the other's rights, and a borrowing or lending of it may amount to so treating it if, but only if, the borrowing or lending is for a period and the circumstances making it equivalent to an outright taking or disposal."

Thus theft is committed where a person borrows a book from a public library and then decides to keep it.

For purposes of theft, property can belong to another even though that person is not aware of its existence if he controls the place where the property is located. R v Woodman (1974).

In two cases, the intention to permanently deprive the owner is not required:

(1) It is an arrestable offence where a person, without having the consent of the owner or other lawful authority, takes any conveyance for his own or another's use or knowing that any conveyance has been taken without such authority, drives it or allows himself to be carried in or on it (Section 12(1)). Both driver and passengers therefore commit an offence under this section. There must be some movement however slight, before the offence

is committed (R v Bogacks 1973). Conveyance includes transport for land, water or air. It is a summary offence to take a pedal cycle.
(2) Where a building is open to the public to view the building or any part of it, or a collection housed in it, it shall be an offence for any person without lawful authority to remove from the building or its grounds the whole or part of any article displayed or kept for display thereon (Section 11).

The maximum sentence for theft is ten years imprisonment.

ROBBERY

When an act of theft is accompanied by violence or the threat of violence it is an offence of robbery. Section 8 of the Theft Act provides:

"A person is guilty of robbery if he steals, and immediately before or at the time of doing so, and in order to do so, he uses force on any person or seeks to put any person in fear of being then and there subjected to force."

N.B. The force need not be applied to the person from whom the stealing takes place. Therefore violence towards a cashier in order to persuade the manager to hand over a sum of money is still robbery.

The maximum sentence for robbery is life-imprisonment.

BURGLARY

A person is guilty of burglary if:
(a) He enters a building as a trespasser with intent to commit any of the following offences: stealing anything in the building or part of the building in question, inflicting on any person therein any grievous bodily harm, or raping any woman therein; or doing unlawful damage to the building or anything therein, or
(b) having entered any building or part of a building as a trespasser he steals or attempts to steal anything in the building or that part of it or inflicts or attempts to inflict on any person therein any grievous bodily harm.

The term building includes an inhabited vehicle or vessel whether or not the person having a habitation there is present.

A person cannot be convicted of burglary under Section 9(1) of the Theft

Act unless he must have known that he was a trespasser or was at the very least, reckless as to whether or not he was entering unlawfully. (R v Collins 1972).

The maximum punishment for burglary is 14 years imprisonment.

Aggravated burglary

Section 10 provides that this offence is committed if at the time of the burglary the accused has with him any firearm or any other offensive weapon, loaded or unloaded, real or imitation.

The maximum punishment for aggravated burglary is life-imprisonment.

OBTAINING BY DECEPTION

Section 15 of the Theft Act provides:

"A person who by any deception dishonestly obtains property belonging to another, with the intention of permanently depriving the other of it, shall on conviction on indictment be liable to imprisonment for a term not exceeding ten years."

Deception is defined by the Act as any deception whether deliberate or reckless by words or conduct as to fact or as to law. See R v McCall (1971).

OBTAINING PECUNIARY ADVANTAGE BY DECEPTION

Section 16 provides:

"A person who by any deception, dishonestly obtains for himself or another any pecuniary advantage shall on conviction on indictment be liable to imprisonment for a term not exceeding five years."

Offences covered by this section would apply to such events as pretending to have a university degree in order to obtain a job, obtaining an overdraft by misrepresenting the purpose for which the money is required, or obtaining discounts by pretending to be a member of a Student's Union.

On a charge of dishonestly obtaining a pecuniary advantage by deception, contrary to Section 16(1) of the Theft Act 1968, the test of dishonesty will be the subjective one of the state of mind of the defendant at the time of committing the offence. Where the defendant contends, therefore, that he had a genuine belief that he could pay a debt, it will be a misdirection to direct the jury that they cannot find there was such a belief unless there were reasonable grounds for it. R v Waterfall (1969).

A person who creates a debt is guilty of obtaining a pecuniary advantage by deception under the Theft Act 1968 Section 16(1) only if that debt is one for which he makes himself liable or is or might become liable (R v Royle 1971).

In order to establish an offence under Section 16 of the Theft Act 1968 it is necessary to show that the deception which was practised was effective in securing for the offender the pecuniary advantage which he obtained (Davis v Flackett 1973).

A person who goes into a restaurant and consumes a meal, intending to pay, but who later decides to leave without paying, and does so, practises a deception and may be convicted of obtaining a pecuniary advantage contrary to Section 16 of the Theft Act 1968 (D.P.P. v Ray 1974).

A person who gives a worthless cheque in payment of a debt evades the debt within Section 16(2) of the Theft Act and may therefore be convicted of obtaining a pecuniary advantage by deception contrary to Section 16(1). D.P.P. v Turner (1974).

Under the Theft Act 1968 Section 16(1) it is not necessary that the person deceived should suffer any loss as a result of the deception, provided that there is some causal connection between the deception and the pecuniary advantage obtained (R v Kovacs 1974).

BLACKMAIL

Section 21 provides:

"A person is guilty of blackmail if, with a view to gain for himself, or another or with intent to cause loss to another, he makes any unwarranted demand with menaces."

The Court of Appeal has indicated that menaces are words or conduct which are likely to operate on the mind of a person of ordinary courage and firmness so as to make him accede unwillingly to a demand. See R v Harry (1974).

HANDLING STOLEN GOODS

Section 22 provides:

"A person handles stolen goods if (otherwise than in the course of stealing) knowing or believing them to be stolen goods he dishonestly receives the goods, or dishonestly undertakes or assists in their retention, removal, disposal or realisation by or for the benefit of another person, or if he arranges to do so."

Handling requires the goods to have been stolen, this covers goods obtained by blackmail or deception.

The maximum punishment for handling is 14 years imprisonment.

CRIMINAL DAMAGE

The offence of criminal damage, formerly called "malicious damage" is covered by the Criminal Damage Act 1971.

Criminal Damage falls into three main classes.

(1) A person who without lawful excuse destroys or damages any property belonging to another, intending to destroy or damage such property, or being reckless as to whether any such property would be destroyed or damaged is guilty of an offence. Section 1(1).

(2) A person who without lawful excuse destroys or damages any property, whether belonging to himself or another
   (a) intending to destroy or damage any property or being reckless as to whether any property would be destroyed or damaged: and
   (b) intending by the destruction or damage to endanger the life of another or being reckless as to whether the life of another would be thereby endangered; shall be guilty of an offence. Section 1(2).

(3) An offence committed under this section by destroying or damaging property by fire shall be charged as arson. Section 1(3).

Section 2 of the Act covers threats.

"A person who without lawful excuse makes to another a threat intending that that other would fear it would be carried out
   (a) to destroy or damage any property belonging to that other or a third person, or

(b) to destroy or damage his own property in a way which he knows is likely to endanger the life of that other or a third person;
shall be guilty of an offence.

It is also an offence to have custody of anything intending to use it, or to cause or permit another to use it to do criminal damage.

There is also an offence of possessing an explosive under the Explosive Substances Act 1883.

MISCELLANEOUS

Trade description

Section 3 of the Trade Descriptions Act 1965 defines a false trade description as a trade description which is false to a material degree, i.e. concerning such matters as quantity, method of manufacture, fitness for purpose, place or date of manufacture. Any person who in the course of a trade or business applies a false trade description to any goods, or who supplies or offers to supply any goods to which a false trade description is applied is guilty of an offence.

Unsolicited goods and services

The Unsolicited Goods and Services Act 1971 provides that if one person delivers unsolicited (neither ordered nor asked for) goods to another with a view to the latter acquiring them or hiring them, then if the sender does not within six months retrieve the goods he is deemed to have made an unconditional gift of them to the recipient.

The Act makes it a criminal offence to:
(a) demand payment for unsolicited goods
(b) send unsolicited publications or advertisements for such publications describing or illustrating sexual techniques
(c) demand payment for the entry of a person's name or other details in a directory without having obtained that person's signature on a note giving details of the directory, and having supplied him with a copy of the note.

OFFENCES AGAINST PUBLIC ORDER

Riot — unlawful assembly — rout

A **riot** at common law is a misdemeanour punishable with imprisonment. The elements essential to constitute a common law riot are:
(1) The presence of not less than three persons.
(2) A common purpose.
(3) Execution or attempted execution of the common purpose.
(4) An intent to help one another, by force if necessary against anyone who may oppose them in the execution of the common purpose.
(5) Force or violence displayed in such a manner as to alarm at least one person of reasonable firmness.

The enterprise must be of a private nature, not directed against the Crown or the State, otherwise the offence might be treason, or treason-felony, or sedition.

If after assembling, the persons concerned do not proceed to execute their purpose, it is only an **unlawful assembly.**

If they attempt to execute their purpose, but do not in fact execute it, it is called a **rout**.

In the Garden House Hotel case (1970), Lord Justice Sachs said that an assembly became unlawful when the crowd, however peaceful their original intention, came together to act for some common purpose in such a way as to make reasonable citizens fear a breach of the peace. It became riotous when alarming force or violence began to be used and, he commented:

"Anyone who actively encouraged such an assembly by words, signs or actions, or by participation in it, was guilty of an offence."

An affray

In R v Sumners (1972) and R v Taylor (1973) the Court of Appeal approved the definition of an affray as follows:

The elements of affray are
(1) fighting by one or more persons without actual violence
(2) in such a manner that reasonable people might be frightened or intimidated (R v Sharp and Johnson 1957).

The importance of the distinction between riot and other serious offences involving disorder is that the police authority have to make good the damage done in riots.

CRIMINAL LAW

The police may arrest without warrant anyone guilty of riot, rout, unlawful assembly, affray or any other disturbance of the public peace. Any person arrested may be bound over to keep the peace, or committed for trial.

Treason

Treason Act 1351

"Item, whereas diverse opinions have been before this time in what case treason shall be said, and in what not; the King, at the request of the Lords and of the commons hath made a declaration in the manner as hereafter followeth, that is to say, when a man doth compass or imagine the death of our lord the King, or of our lady his Queen, or of their eldest son and heir; or if a man do violate the King's companion, or the King's eldest daughter unmarried, or the wife of the King's eldest son and heir; or if a man do levy war against our lord the King in his realm, or be adherent to the King's enemies in his realm, giving to them aid and comfort in the realm or elsewhere, and thereby be probably attainted of open deed by the people of their condition and if a man sley the chancellor, treasurer, or the King's justices of the one bench or the other, justices in eyre or justices of assise, and all other justices assigned to hear and determine, being in their places, doing their offices: and it is to be understood that in the cases above rehearsed, that ought to be judged treason which extends to our lord the King, and his royal majesty ..."

Treason is therefore the most serious crime against the security of the State and is comparatively rare, the most famous cases being those of Sir Roger Casement and William Joyce (Joyce v D.P.P. 1946).

Treason is still a capital offence.

Treason Act 1702, Treason Act 1795 and Treason Act 1814: Any knowledge and concealment of treason is called misprision of treason and has always been a common law misdemeanour.

In 1848 Parliament created the offence of treason-felony as juries were becoming reluctant to convict people charged with treason as it carried the death penalty. Treason-felony consists of any of the three following acts which are punishable by imprisonment for life.
  (1) "Compassing" to deprive or depose the Sovereign of her Kingdom or any other of her Dominions.
  (2) Levying war against the Sovereign within the United Kingdom in

SPECIFIC OFFENCES

order by force or constraint to compel her to change her measures, or to intimidate or overawe Parliament.
(3) Stirring up any foreigner with force to invade the United Kingdom or any other part of the Sovereign's dominions.

Sedition

May be in writing or by spoken words. It consists of an attempt to vilify or degrade the Queen in the eyes of her subjects, or to create discontent or disaffection, or to incite people to tumult, violence and disorder, or bring the Government of this country or the Constitution into hatred and contempt, or to effect any change in the laws by the recommendations of physical force. People taking even a passive role at a meeting where sedition is preached may be guilty of the offence.

Fair comment is tolerated in England and people have the right to meet and express their opinions so the offence of sedition will only be committed when written or spoken words exceed the bounds of fair and reasonable argument or discussion.

Incitement to disaffection

The Act of 1934 states that, if any person maliciously and advisedly endeavours to seduce any members of His Majesty's forces from his duty or allegiance to His Majesty, he shall be guilty of an offence under this Act.

Treason Act 1702

Section 3 provides that it is treason by overt act to attempt to hinder the next successor to the Crown from succeeding.

The crime was further extended by

Treason Act 1795 Section 1

"If any person or persons whatsoever shall, within the realm or without, compass, imagine, invent, devise, or intend death or destruction, or any bodily harm tending to death or destruction, maim or wounding, imprisonment or restraint, of the person of His Majesty, His heirs, and successors ... and such compassings, imaginations, inventions, devices, or intentions, or any of them, shall express, utter or declare, by publishing any printing or writing or by any overt act or deed; lawful and credible witnesses, upon trial or otherwise convicted or attainted by due course of law, then every such person and persons, so as aforesaid offending, shall be deemed, declared and adjudged to be a traitor and traitors, and shall suffer pains of death ... as in cases of high treason."

Treason Act 1814 Section 1

"In all cases of high treason the sentence or judgement to be pronounced or awarded from and after the passing of this Act against any person convicted or adjudged guilty shall be that such person shall be hanged by the neck until such person be dead."

Incitement to Mutiny Act 1797

"From and after the passing of this Act, any person who shall maliciously and advisedly endeavour to seduce any person or persons serving in His Majesty's forces by sea or land from his or their duty and allegiance to His Majesty, or to incite or stir up any such person or persons to commit any act of mutiny, or to make or endeavour to make any mutinous assembly, or to commit any traitorous or mutinous practice whatsoever, shall, on being legally convicted of such offence be adjudged guilty of felony."

Official secrets

By the Official Secrets Acts 1911 and 1913
(1) "A person who for any purpose prejudicial to the safety or interests of the State,
 (a) approaches, inspects, passes over or is in the neighbourhood of or enters any prohibited place; or
 (b) makes any sketch, plan, model or note which is calculated to or might be or is intended to be directly or indirectly useful to any enemy or potential enemy; or
 (c) obtains, collects, records or publishes or communicates to any other person any secret official code word or pass word or any sketch, plan, model, article, or note or other document or information which is calculated to be or might be directly or indirectly useful to an enemy

 is guilty of an offence punishable by imprisonment for 14 years."
(2) "A person who has in his control any information mentioned in paragraph 1(c) which relates to a prohibited place or has been obtained in contravention of the Official Secrets Acts or has been entrusted in confidence to him by any person holding office under Her Majesty or which he has obtained as a result of service under or a contract with Her Majesty, and
 (a) communicates the information to an unauthorised person; or

(b) uses the information for the benefit of any foreign power or in any manner prejudicial to the safety of the State; or
(c) retains a document etc., in his possession when he has no right to do so, or
(d) fails to take reasonable care of such a document etc.
is guilty of an offence punishable by imprisonment for two years."

Firearms and offensive weapons

By the Firearms Act 1968, a person who makes or attempts to make any use whatsoever of a firearm or imitation firearm, with intent to resist or prevent the lawful arrest or detention of himself or any other person, commits an offence punishable with imprisonment for 14 years. Such punishment may be additional to that awarded for the offence for which the accused was being arrested.

By the same Act, a person who, at the time of committing or being arrested for any of the offences specified in the first Schedule to the Act has in his possession a firearm or imitation firearm may be sentenced to seven years imprisonment in addition to the penalty for the specified offence unless he shows that his possession of the firearm was for a lawful purpose.

By the Prevention of Crimes Act 1953, any person without lawful authority or reasonable excuse, the proof whereof shall be on him, has with him in any public place any offensive weapon is guilty of an offence punishable on summary conviction by three months imprisonment, a fine of £50 or both, and on indictment, a fine of £100 or both.

By the Theft Act 1968 Section 10:

A person is guilty of aggravated burglary if he commits any burglary and at the time has with him any firearm or imitation firearm, any weapon of offence, or any explosive, and for this purpose
- (a) "Firearm" includes an airgun or air pistol, and "imitation" firearm means anything which has the appearance of being a firearm, whether capable of being discharged or not; and
- (b) "Weapon of offence" means any article made or adapted for use for causing injury to or incapacitating a person, or intended by the person having it with him for such use; and
- (c) "explosive" means any article manufactured for the purpose of producing a practical effect by explosion, or intended by the person having it with him for that purpose.

A person guilty of aggravated burglary shall on conviction on indictment be liable to imprisonment for life.

Obscene publications

Section 1 of the 1959 Act provides: "For the purposes of this Act an article shall be deemed to be obscene if its effect ... is, if taken as a whole, such as to tend to deprave and corrupt persons who are likely, having regard to all relevant circumstances, to read, see or **hear** the matter contained or embodied in it."

Section 2(1), as amended in the 1964 Act, provides that "subject as hereinafter provided, any person who publishes an obscene article for gain or not, for himself or another ... shall be liable on summary conviction or on conviction on indictment to a fine or imprisonment."

Section 4 reads: "(1) A person shall not be convicted of an offence against Section 2 of this Act ... if it is proved that publication of the article in question is justified as being **for the public good** on the ground that it is in the interests of science, literature, art or learning, or other objects of general concern. (2) It is hereby declared that the opinion of experts as to the literary, artistic, scientific or other merits of an article may be admitted in any proceedings under this Act either to establish or to negative the said ground."

In D.P.P. v Jordan reported in "The Times" 18 November 1976 it was held that expert evidence is not admissible in support of the defence under Section 4 − where the evidence is to the effect that pornographic material is psychologically beneficial to persons with certain sexual tendencies in that it relieves their sexual tensions and may divert them from anti-social activities.

Lord Wilberforce approved the course commonly taken of directing the jury first to consider the tendency of the material under Section 1 then to consider the merits under Section 4, and finally to weigh one against the other. DW(C) 11.1977

Perjury

The Perjury Act 1911 states:

"If any person lawfully sworn as a witness or as an interpreter in a judicial proceeding wilfully makes a statement material in that proceeding, which he knows to be false or does not believe to be true, he shall be guilty of perjury, and shall, on conviction thereof on indictment, be liable to imprisonment for a term not exceeding seven years or to a fine or to both such imprisonment and fine."

The expression "judicial proceeding" includes a proceeding before any court, tribunal, or person having by law power to hear, receive and examine evidence on oath.

The question whether a statement on which perjury is assigned was material is a question of law to be determined by the court of trial.

It is sufficient to support a charge of perjury that it can be proved by the evidence of more than one witness that the accused made statements on other occasions which were different from those which he made on oath (R v Hook 1858).

A person is not guilty of perjury if, having been sworn, he knowingly makes a false statement before a tribunal which is not properly constituted.

Other statements covered by the Act are:
(1) False statements with reference to marriage. It is an offence to make a false oath, make or sign a false declaration, make a false entry in any register of marriage, knowingly and wilfully.
(2) False statements as to births or deaths. It is an offence wilfully to falsely answer any questions put by a registrar or wilfully to give any false information concerning any birth or death.
(3) False statutory declarations and other false statements without oath. If any person knowingly and wilfully makes (otherwise than on oath) a statement false in a material particular and the statement is made
   (a) in a statutory declaration, or
   (b) in an abstract, account, balance sheet, book certificate declaration, entry, estimate, inventory, notice, report, return, or other document which he is authorised or required to make, attest, or verify, by any public general Act of Parliament for the time being in force, or
   (c) in any oral declaration or oral answer which he is required to make by, under, or in pursuance of any public general Act of Parliament for the time being in force

he shall be guilty of a misdemeanour and shall be liable on conviction thereof on indictment to imprisonment, with or without hard labour, for any term not exceeding two years, or to a fine or both such imprisonment and fine. (A penalty which of course has been changed.)

THE CRIMINAL PROCESS

ARREST

Arrest simply means imposing a restraint on a person's liberty.

If a person is detained in custody, he or someone acting on his behalf may apply for a writ of habeas corpus against the person detaining him. The person responsible for the detention will be required to appear in court to justify the detention of the prisoner. The application for a writ is usually made to a Divisional Court of the High Court or if no court is in session to a single judge.

The police have no right to detain anyone merely to help them with their enquiries.

The police may lawfully arrest anyone whom they reasonably suspect of having committed an arrestable offence, even though no such offence has in fact been committed.

For a private citizen's arrest to be lawful, an offence must actually have been committed at the time of arrest.

A person must be told the reason for his arrest unless it is obvious.

Arrest on warrant

A warrant is an order of a magistrate requiring the police to whom it is addressed to arrest the person whose name appears on the warrant and then bring him before the court. The warrant may be backed for bail which means the person may be released on undertakings that he will appear at court.

After arrest, police interrogation must comply with the Judges' Rules. Under these rules a police officer must caution the suspect, invite him to make a statement under caution, must not prompt or give any other assistance to the suspect, must inform him of any charge and again give a

THE CRIMINAL PROCESS

caution. The Rules also give an arrested person the right to communicate with and consult privately with a solicitor.

JUDGES' RULES 1964

As a preamble to the Rules, Home Office circular No 89 of 1978 states that the Rules do not affect the principles:
(a) That citizens have a duty to help a police officer to discover and apprehend offenders;
(b) That police officers, otherwise than by arrest, cannot compel any person against his will to come or remain in any police station;
(c) That every person at any stage of an investigation should be able to communicate and to consult privately with a solicitor. This is so even if he is in custody provided that in such a case no unreasonable delay or hindrance is caused to the process of investigation or the administration of justice by his doing so;
(d) That when a police officer who is making enquiries of any person about an offence has enough evidence to prefer a charge against that person for the offence, he should without delay cause that person to be charged or informed that he may be prosecuted for the offence;
(e) That it is a fundamental condition of the admissibility in evidence against any person, equally of any oral answer given by that person to a question put by a police officer and of any statement made by that person, that it shall have been voluntary, in the sense that it has not been obtained from him by fear of or by oppression.

The principle set out in paragraph (e) is overriding and applicable in all cases. Within that principle the following Rules are put forward as a guide to police officers conducting investigations. Non-conformity with these Rules may render answers and statements liable to be excluded from evidence in subsequent criminal proceedings.

The text of the 1964 Rules
1. When a police officer is trying to discover whether or by whom, an offence has been committed he is entitled to question any person, whether suspected or not, from whom he thinks that useful information may be obtained.

This is so whether or not the person in question has been taken into custody, so long as he has not been charged with the offence, or informed that he may be prosecuted.

N.B. The use of the word offence entitles the officer to question even in cases of minor breaches of the law.

2. As soon as a police officer has evidence which would afford reasonable grounds for suspecting that a person has committed an offence, he shall caution that person or cause him to be cautioned before putting to him any questions, or further questions, relating to that offence.

The caution shall be in the following terms:

"You are not obliged to say anything unless you wish to do so but what you say may be put into writing and given in evidence."

When, after being cautioned a person is being questioned, or elects to make a statement, a record shall be kept of the time, and place at which any such questioning began and ended and of the persons present.

N.B. To constitute reasonable suspicion, it is not necessary that the police officer should have enough evidence to prefer a charge, it may only be that the suspect had the motive and opportunity to commit a crime.

3. (i) Where a person is charged with or informed that he may be prosecuted for an offence he shall be cautioned in the following terms:

"Do you wish to say anything? You are not obliged to say anything unless you wish to do so, but whatever you say will be taken down in writing and may be given in evidence."

3. (ii) It is only in exceptional cases that questions relating to the offence should be put to the accused person after he has been charged or informed that he may be prosecuted. Such questions may be put where they are necessary for the purpose of preventing or minimising harm or loss to some other person or to the public or for clearing up an ambiguity in a previous answer or statement.

Before any such questions are put the accused should be cautioned in these terms:

"I wish to put some questions to you about the offence with which you have been charged (or about the offence for which you may be prosecuted). You are not obliged to answer any of these questions but if you do the questions and answers will be taken down in writing and may be given in evidence."

Any questions put and answers given relating to the offence must be contemporaneously recorded in full and the record signed by that person or if he refuses by the interrogating officer.

3. (iii) When such a person is being questioned, or elects to make a statement, a record shall be kept of the time and place at which any statement began and ended and of the persons present.

4. All written statements made after caution shall be taken in the following manner:

(a) If a person says that he wants to make a statement he shall be told that it is intended to make a written record of what he says. He shall always be asked whether he wishes to write down himself what he wants to say; if he says that he cannot write or that he would like someone to write it for him, a police officer may offer to write the statement for him. If he accepts the offer the police officer shall, before starting ask the person making the statement to sign, or make his mark to the following:

"I ..., wish to make a statement. I want someone to write down what I say. I have been told that I need not say anything unless I wish to do so and that whatever I say may be given in evidence."

(b) Any person writing his own statement shall be allowed to do so without any prompting as distinct from indicating to him what matters are material.

(c) The person making the statement, if he is going to write it himself, shall be asked to write out and sign before writing what he wants to say, the following:

"I make this statement of my own free will. I have been told that I need not say anything unless I wish to do so and that whatever I say may be given in evidence."

(d) Whenever a police officer writes the statement, he shall take down the exact words spoken by the person making the statement without putting any questions other than such as may be needed to make the statement coherent, intelligible and relevant to the material matters; he shall not prompt him, (i.e. questions may be asked to clarify a time, place, etc).

(e) When the writing of a statement by a police officer is finished the person making it shall be asked to read it and to make any corrections, alterations or additions he wishes. When he has finished reading it he shall be asked to write and sign or make his mark on the following certificate at the end of the statement:

> "I have read the above statement and I have been told that I can correct, alter or add anything I wish. This statement is true. I have made it of my own free will."

(f) If the person who has made a statement refuses to read it or to write the above mentioned certificate at the end of it or to sign it, the senior police officer present shall record on the statement itself and in the presence of the person making it, what has happened. If the person making the statement cannot read or refuses to read it, the officer who has taken it down shall read it over to him and ask him whether he would like to correct, alter or add anything and to put his signature or make his mark at the end. The police officer shall then certify on the statement itself what he has done.

5. If at any time after a person has been charged with, or has been informed that he may be prosecuted for an offence a police officer wishes to bring to the notice of that person any written statement made by another person who in respect of the same offence has also been charged or informed that he may be prosecuted he shall hand to that person a true copy of such written statement, but nothing shall be said or done to invite any reply or comment. If that person says that he would like to make a statement in reply, or starts to say something, he shall at once be cautioned or further cautioned as prescribed by Rule 3(a).

N.B. This rule does not place any obligation upon the police to hand to a person charged statements made by others.

6. Persons other than police officers charged with the duty of investigating offences or charging offenders shall, so far as may be practicable comply with these rules.

This section applies to railway police, customs officers, post office officials and persons appointed to hold inquiries.

BAIL ACT 1976

The defendant need not be granted bail if the court is satisfied that there are substantial grounds for believing that the defendant, if redeemed on bail (whether subject to conditions or not) would

(a) fail to surrender to custody, or
(b) commit an offence while on bail, or

(c) interfere with witnesses or otherwise obstruct the course of justice, whether in relation to himself or any other person.

This applies to defendants accused of imprisonable offences.

In cases of offences not punishable by imprisonment the defendant need not be granted bail if
   (a) it appears to the court that, having been previously granted bail in criminal proceedings, he has failed to surrender to custody, in accordance with his obligations under the grant of bail **and**
   (b) the Court believes, in view of that failure, that the defendant, if released on bail (whether subject to conditions or not) would fail to surrender to custody.

The Court **shall have regard to**
   (a) nature and seriousness of the offence or default (and the probable method of dealing with the defendant for it).
   (b) The character, antecedents, associations and community ties of the defendant.
   (c) The defendant's record as respects the fulfilment of his obligations under previous grants of bail in criminal proceedings.
   (d) The strength of the evidence of his having committed the offence or having defaulted, except in the case of a defendant whose case is adjourned for inquiries or a report.

as well as to any others which appear to be relevant.

Protection for the accused

Where a Magistrates' Court or Crown Court
   (a) withholds bail in criminal proceedings, or
   (b) imposes conditions in granting bail in criminal proceeding, or
   (c) varies any conditions of bail

the Court shall with a view to enabling the defendant to consider making an application in the matter to another court give reasons for withholding bail or imposing or varying the conditions.

PUNISHMENTS AND OTHER ORDERS OF A CRIMINAL COURT

The purpose of punishment is fourfold:

1. **Retribution** – to pay the criminal back for his crime and demonstrate that crime does not pay.
2. **Prevention** – To protect the public. By imprisoning an offender, he is prevented from committing further offences.
3. **Reform** – The offender must be regarded as a member of society and efforts made to reform him.
4. **Deterrence** – The punishment should be such as to deter the offender from repeating the offence and also deter other members of society from emulating his deeds.

Custodial or semi-custodial sentences

1. Imprisonment

The court has to be satisfied that there is no other satisfactory method of dealing with the offender. For persons under 21, unless the court considers that the appropriate sentence is less than six months, or more than two years, Borstal should be used in preference to prison.

If several offences arise out of the same set of circumstances, the sentences should be concurrent, in other words, run together, i.e. three concurrent sentences of six months means the total length of imprisonment would be six months.

If separate offences are involved, then the sentences may be consecutive, i.e. three consecutive sentences of six months would mean a total of 18 months imprisonment.

Some prisons are "open" that is reserved for non-violent prisoners and supervision in such prisons is at a minimum. Other prisons are "closed". In these prisons, supervision is strict and conditions are usually grossly overcrowded.

Persons suffering from insanity or sentenced to be detained during Her Majesty's Pleasure are detained in a Mental Hospital.

Most statutes lay down maximum punishment for particular offences; robbery and arson for example are punishable with life imprisonment. A Crown Court may award any sentence from death (treason) to an absolute discharge but a Magistrates' Court may not sentence a person to more than six months imprisonment for any one offence.

Remission – if a prisoner conducts himself acceptably during his stay in prison up to one-third of his sentence may be remitted.

Parole – A prisoner may apply to the Parole Board after he has served one-third of his sentence or 12 months whichever is the longer. If parole is granted the prisoner is released on licence which can be determined at any time and he is subject to supervision. The system of parole is criticized because the length of imprisonment is decided by the executive and not by the judiciary.

2. Suspended prison sentences

Any court which passes a sentence of imprisonment for a term of not more than two years may order that the sentence be suspended for a period to be specified in the order with the restriction that it should not be for less than one nor more than two years. The effect is that the offender does not go to prison unless he commits an offence of the same type during the period of suspension. In which case he will serve the amount of the suspended sentence in addition to any period of imprisonment imposed for the latter offence.

3. Hospital order

In addition to convicted persons, a hospital order may be made by the court where it is found that the offender is suffering from mental illness or severe abnormality without first convicting him if satisfied that the accused did the act charged. The purpose of the order is to enable the offender to be compulsorily detained, or placed under guardianship, for as long as is necessary in his and the public interest (Mental Health Act 1959).

4. Borstal

Young persons and offenders between 15 and 21 may be sentenced to a period of borstal training. The sentence is indeterminate and involves training for a period of not less than six months and not more than two years. The offender is given a target date for release on his arrival at the training borstal and his actual release date depends upon the recommendation of the Board of Visitors to the Home Office. After release, the trainee is under supervision for a period of two years and is liable to be recalled for misbehaving.

The object of a borstal sentence is to provide training for young people who find difficulty in settling down in society. As with prisons, these are closed institutions involving a high degree of security and used for more serious offenders than open institutions which have a more relaxed atmosphere and provide greater scope for training. Great emphasis is placed on physical and educational training.

Borstal training can normally only be imposed by the Crown Court.

5. Detention centres

A male offender between the ages of 17 and 21 may be committed to a detention centre for a period of between three and six months for a period of intensive training.

Offenders aged between 14 and 17 may be sent to a detention centre for three months. After such sentence there is a period of one year's supervision and the offender may be recalled for bad behaviour.

It is customary to give automatic remission of one month on detention centre sentences and as the normal sentence is three months, a two-month sentence is usually served. Such remission may however be forfeit for bad behaviour.

6. Attendance centres

These centres are for persons over 10 and under 21, found guilty of a breach of a probation or supervision order or failure to pay a fine or of an offence punishable in the case of an adult by imprisonment. The offender is ordered to attend for a specified number of hours, normally twelve, spread over a number of weeks for character training. The offender will be obliged to do physical training, chores and hobbies usually under the supervision of a police officer.

7. Care orders

These orders are made by a court where a child or young person is in need of care, protection or control, or has committed a criminal offence. The order is a decision by the juvenile court that a child is in need of care and control which it is unlikely to receive unless such an order is made. The local authority is bound to review the order every six months and the child's parents have power to require the authority to justify the continuation of the order by applying to the juvenile court to discharge it.

The child may be sent to a community home, which has replaced the old Approved Schools and Remand Homes, at which it will receive a full-time education either within the establishment or at school and live in a more secure and stable environment than at home. Alternatively, it may be boarded out at a foster-home and live in a settled environment.

Other forms of sentence

8. Absolute discharge

This order may be made by a court where it finds the accused guilty, but having regard to all the circumstances, thinks it inexpedient to inflict any punishment. Such an order may be made when the accused is technically in breach of the law but he is not morally blameworthy.

9. Conditional discharge

This is similar to an absolute discharge except that the offender is discharged subject to the condition that he commits no offence during a specified period not exceeding three years. If the offender should commit a further offence during the relevant period, he is liable to be punished, both for the further offence and for the original one.

10. Binding-over

From the time of the Justices of the Peace Act 1361, magistrates have had power to require that any persons appearing before them, even as a complainant or a witness, should enter into a recognisance with, or without sureties, to keep the peace and be of good behaviour. The power can also be used in respect of convicted persons and the effect of the binding-over is that the offender stands to forfeit the recognisance if he fails to be of good behaviour or to keep the peace during the stated period.

11. Probation

Is imposed where the court is of the opinion that the offender does not merit a sentence of imprisonment and yet is in need of supervision. The court has general power to require the probationer to comply with such requirements as it considers necessary for securing the good conduct of the offender or for preventing a repetition by him of the same offence or the commission of other offences. The order may be for a period of between six months and three years and if the conditions of the order are broken or a further offence committed during this period, the probationer may be recalled for sentence on the original charge.

A probation order may be varied or a conditonal discharge substituted by either the supervising court or the court which made the order if the probationer's response to the order is such that discharge or variation is appropriate.

12. Fine

This is the imposition of the payment of a sum of money to the court for an offence committed. The maximum fine which can be imposed is usually specified in the statute creating the offence. In other cases there is a general limit of £1,000 on fines imposed by magistrates' courts.

The court must allow a stated period in which to pay the fine unless
(1) the offender appears to have the means to pay at once, or
(2) it seems that he is unlikely to remain in the United Kingdom, or
(3) the court proposes to pass an immediate sentence for some other offence or he is serving such a sentence.

13. Compensation order

A court may order a person convicted of an offence to pay compensation for any personal injury, loss or damage resulting from that offence or from any other offence which is taken into consideration by the court in determining sentence. The maximum compensation awardable in a Magistrates' Court is £1,000 for any one offence.

14. Bankruptcy

A court may make a criminal bankruptcy order where, as a result of an offence of which a person has been convicted, either standing alone or with other relevant offences, loss or damage has been suffered by persons whose identity is known to the court and the loss or damage exceeds £15,000. The object of the order is to prevent criminals enjoying the fruits of their crime after release.

15. Deferred sentence

By Section 1 of the Powers of Criminal Courts Act 1973, both the Crown Court and the Magistrates' Court may, with the consent of the offender, defer passing sentence for one period of not more than six months. This power is intended to give the offender a chance to show the court that his promise of reformation is made in earnest.

16. Community service order

A person over 17 may be required to perform community service of not more than 240 hours of unpaid work, usually at week-ends. There are certain conditions: the offender must be a suitable person, arrangements must exist in the area where he lives for such work to be undertaken, he must consent to such order being made, and the order must be fulfilled within 12 months. The sort of work undertaken by persons subject to such orders includes improving amenities, helping the aged and disabled, gardening and cleaning hospitals. One lady so enjoyed her community service work that she continued playing the piano at an old folk's home long after her compulsory period had ended.

JURIES AND THE JUDICIARY

A jury is a body of 12 people who sit in both criminal and civil courts to decide matters of fact in a case as opposed to the judge who decides matters of law.

Under the Juries Act 1974 qualifications for jury service are that a person must:
(1) be on the electoral register
(2) be between the ages of 18 and 65
(3) be resident in the U.K. for at least 5 years since attaining the age of 13.

Persons ineligible for jury service are members of the judiciary, others concerned with the administration of justice, the clergy and those mentally ill.

Persons who have served a prison sentence of three months or more are disqualified for ten years and persons who have been sentenced to prison for five years or more are disqualified for life.

Excusal from jury service may be claimed by doctors, MPs and members of the armed forces.

COMPOSITION OF JURIES

Criminal jury

The Petty Jury, the forerunner of the present system, was introduced by the Lateran Council of 1215. Today the criminal jury is found in the Central Criminal Court and the Crown Courts. The sworn duty of the jury is "to well and truly try the case and give a true verdict according to the evidence". The defence may challenge up to three members of a jury without giving reasons, any further challenge must be supported by reasons (Juries Act 1974).

Under the Criminal Justice Act 1967 a majority verdict may be allowed if:
(1) the jury has deliberated for 2 hours or more
(2) in a jury of 11 or more jurors ten at least agree
(3) in a case where there are ten jurors, nine agree.

If a juror dies or is ill, provided both sides agree and the number of jurors is not reduced below ten, the case may continue and a verdict be given.

Coroners jury

Consists of 7–11 persons who assist in an inquiry into sudden death, death by violence, death in suspicious circumstances, or death in prison. The coroner may accept a majority verdict provided that there are not more than two dissentients.

Advantages and disadvantages of trial by jury

Advantages

(1) A verdict by one's peers seems more acceptable than the verdict of a judge.
(2) Lay people are involved in the administration of justice.
(3) The general public has confidence in jury trials.
(4) As the judge has to explain facts to the jury, justice is seen to be done.
(5) A jury has no direct interest in the result of the trial.

Disadvantages

(1) Juries may not be competent to understand the evidence, especially in cases of fraud.
(2) Juries may be swayed by experienced and eloquent counsel.
(3) Some juries are prone to leniency.
(4) Local prejudice may exist in some trials.
(5) Threats, intimidation, and corruption may influence some jurors.
(6) Long trials cause hardship to jurors, especially self-employed.
(7) Jurors of 18 may be too inexperienced to determine guilt or innocence.

"The trial judge or jury must learn about facts from witnesses who being humanly fallible, frequently make mistakes in observations of what

CRIMINAL LAW

they saw and heard, or in their recollections of what they observed, or in the courtroom report of those recollections.

Some hidden, unconscious biases of trial judges or jurors, such as, for example, plus or minus reactions to women, or unmarried women, or red-haired women, or brunettes, or men with deep voices, or high pitched voices, or fidgety men, or men who wear thick eye-glasses, or those who have pronounced gestures or nervous tics — biases of which no-one can be aware.

The chief obstacle to prophesying a trial-court decision is, then, the inability, thanks to these inscrutable factors, to foresee what a particular trial judge or jury will believe to be the facts — legal writers often overlook these difficulties, and one might chide them for forgetting **juriesprudence** or **magistrates prudence** or **judges prudence**."

Jerome Frank in "Law and the Modern Mind"

CHALLENGING THE JURY

(1) Either side may challenge the array (the whole body of jurors) on the ground that the person responsible for summoning the jurors in question is biased or has acted improperly. Juries Act 1974 Section 12(6).

(2) Either side may challenge individual jurors for cause, that is because the juror is disqualified or ineligible or because he is partial or might be partial. This is known as a challenge for favour.

(3) Each defendant has the right to make three peremptory challenges, that is he need give no reason for the challenge. (Juries Act 1974 as amended by Criminal Law Act 1977.)

(4) The prosecution may require that individual jurors should stand by, that is be excluded unless it is impossible to form a jury from the panel of prospective jurors without calling on them.

Normally a sufficient number of persons is summoned to prepare for all challenges, but if a jury of 12 cannot be found the ancient custom of "praying a tales" may be resorted to, i.e. any qualified person in the vicinity of the court may be summoned to attend jury service.

LEGAL AID IN CRIMINAL PROCEEDINGS

Legal aid in defending criminal charges began with the passing of the Poor Prisoners' Defence Act 1903 but such legal aid only applied to cases tried on indictment at quarter sessions and assizes.

The Poor Prisoners' Defence Act 1930, provided a more comprehensive system of financial aid which covered committal and summary proceedings and trials on indictment.

The current law on the grant of legal aid in criminal proceedings is provided by the Legal Aid Act 1974, and the principal occasions when legal aid is available are as follows:

(1) **Magistrates' Court proceedings** – legal aid can be obtained on application to the court. It can be granted by the clerk but can only be refused by magistrates.

(2) **Crown Court proceedings** – legal aid can be granted either by the Magistrates' Court committing the defendant to Crown Court, or from whom the appeal has been taken, or by the Crown Court. This order covers advice on appeal to the Court of Appeal.

(3) **Judge in chambers** – bail: can only be obtained in practice through the services of the Official Solicitor who then acts for the applicant.

(4) **Court of Appeal** – can only be obtained through the single judge or full court. Usually the Registrar of the Criminal Division of the Court is directed to act for the appellant.

(5) **Case stated to High Court** and application for prerogative orders – legal aid in such cases is available under the civil scheme.

In deciding whether to make a legal aid order the court has to consider:

(1) the nature of the charge to determine if it warrants legal aid,
(2) the means of the defendant.

The recommendations of the Widgery Committee (1966) were that legal aid should be granted provided that the applicant's means (or lack of them) justified it in the following circumstances:

(1) where the charge is a grave one in the sense that the accused is in real danger of losing his liberty or livelihood or suffering serious damage to his reputation or

(2) where a charge raises a substantial question of law; or

(3) where the accused is unable to follow the proceedings and state his own case because of his inadequate knowledge of English, mental illness or because of other mental or physical disability, or

(4) where the nature of the defence involves the tracing and interviewing of witnesses or expert cross-examination of a witness for the prosecution, or
(5) where legal representation is desirable in the interests of someone other than the accused as, for example, in the case of sexual offences against young children where it is undesirable that the accused should cross-examine the witness in person.

Under the provisions of the Powers of Criminal Courts Act 1973 Section 20(1), it is now unlawful for any court to send an unrepresented defendant to prison, borstal or a detention centre for the first time unless he has been specifically informed of his right to apply for legal aid and has been given an opportunity to do so, and has refused, or failed to apply or had his application refused on the grounds of his means.

Under the Legal Aid Act 1974 Section 2(4), a magistrates' court may assign a solicitor present in court to assist an unrepresented defendant.

Refusal to grant legal aid can be challenged by applying to the Divisional Court for review.

THE JUDICIARY

The Judiciary is a collective name for the body of judges who preside over our courts. Judges are appointed by the Queen and except for circuit judges and recorders, may only be removed on an address from both Houses of Parliament. Circuit judges and recorders may be removed by the Lord Chancellor for misconduct.

The Lord Chancellor is appointed by the Queen on the advice of the Prime Minister. His position combines duties which are legislative, executive, and judicial; it is therefore an exception to the constitutional doctrine of the "Separation of Powers". He is head of the Judiciary, President of the House of Lords as an appellate court and President of the Supreme Court. He is the most important member of the Judicial Committee of the Privy Council and is head of the Chancery Division of the High Court. He appoints puisne judges of the High Court, Circuit Judges and Recorders, and Magistrates and also approves the appointments of legally qualified chairmen of certain administrative tribunals.

The Lord Chief Justice. Also appointed by the Queen on the advice of the Prime Minister. He is head of the Q.B.D. of the High Court and head of the Court of Appeal.

The Master of the Rolls. Appointed by the Queen on the advice of the Prime Minister. He is deputy to the Lord Chancellor and for practical purposes is head of the Court of Appeal. He supervises the admission of solicitors to the Rolls of the Supreme Court.

President of the Family Division. Is appointed by the Queen on the advice of the Prime Minister and is responsible for the work of the Family Division of the High Court.

Lords of Appeal in Ordinary. Known as "Law Lords" are appointed by the Queen on the advice of the Prime Minister from existing judges of at least two years standing or from barristers of at least fifteen years standing – usually appointment is from the ranks of Lord Justices of Appeal.

Lord Justices of Appeal are appointed by the Queen on the advice of the Prime Minister from barristers of at least fifteen years standing or from the existing body of puisne judges. They are judges of the Court of Appeal.

Puisne Judges (High Court Judges). Appointed by the Queen on the advice of the Lord Chancellor from barristers of at least ten years standing. They hold office "whilst of good behaviour" and can only be removed from their judicial office by a resolution of both Houses of Parliament. Puisne Judges must retire at 75 unless they were in office in 1958.

Circuit Judges. Appointed by the Queen on the advice of the Lord Chancellor, from barristers of ten years standing or recorders who have held judicial office for at least five years. In this way it is possible for a solicitor to become a circuit judge. The retiring age is 72, although a circuit judge may be asked to stay in office until he is 75. A circuit judge may be removed by the Lord Chancellor on the grounds of "incapacity or misbehaviour".

Recorders are part-time judges expected to serve a minimum of 30 days a year. They are appointed from barristers or solicitors of at least ten years standing by the Queen on the advice of the Lord Chancellor. The compulsory retiring age is 75 and the appointment may be terminated for incapacity or misconduct.

The law officers

The law officers are the Attorney-General and the Solicitor-General. Both are appointed by the Queen on the advice of the Prime Minister and the appointments are political.

The Attorney-General's duties are:
(1) To advise the Government on legal matters.
(2) To represent the Crown in civil cases and to act as prosecutor in important criminal cases.
(3) Certain criminal offences must be reported to the Attorney-General and his consent is necessary before criminal proceedings may be taken in cases such as bribery, incest, corrupt practices, offences against the Official Secrets Act, the Dangerous Drugs Act 1951, and various other Acts.
(4) He is head of the English bar.
(5) He supervises the work of the Director of Public Prosecutions.

The Solicitor-General is the deputy of the Attorney-General, and has similar duties. He is a barrister and usually a member of the House of Commons. By the Law Officers Act 1944, any function that may be discharged by the Attorney-General may also be carried out by the Solicitor-General, when the former is ill or absent or when the office of Attorney-General is vacant.

The Director of Public Prosecutions is a civil servant who is a barrister or solicitor of at least ten years standing. He acts under the authority of the Attorney-General and he and his department advise the police, magistrates clerks and others enforcing the law on prosecutions in difficult cases. He must prosecute in all offences punishable by death and in cases of murder and manslaughter and may prosecute in cases referred to him by a Government department.

INDEX OF CASES

A   No.
Abbot v R (1976)   69
Attorney-General for Northern Ireland v Gallagher (1963)   21
Atwal v Massey (1971)   65

B
Buckoke v Greater London Council (1971)   12

C
Coward v Baddeley (1859   56
Cundy v Le Cocq (1884)   5

D
Davey v Lee (1968)   33
D.P.P. v Beard (1920)   40
D.P.P. v Morgan (1975)   39
D.P.P. v Newbury and Jones (1976)   22
D.P.P. v Ray (1973)   85
D.P.P. v Smith (1961)   47
D.P.P. v Withers (1974)   80
Duncan v Jones (1936)   63

F
Fagan v Metropolitan Police Commissioner (1968)   55
Fairclough v Whipp (1951)   86
Ferguson v Weaving (1951)   25

G
Gardner v Akeroyd (1952)   31

H

Haughton v Smith (1973)	6
Hill v Baxter (1958)	43
Hyam v D.P.P. (1974)	46

J

Johnson v Phillips (1976)	35
Joyce v D.P.P. (1946)	66

L

Laurence v Metropolitan Police Commissioner (1971)	28

M

McNaghten's Case (1843)	15

R

R v Bailey (1800)	38
R v Blaue (1975)	82
R v Bogacki (1973)	64
R v Bourne (1938)	36
R v Button (1900)	8
R v Casement (1917)	67
R v Church (1966)	45
R v Clarke (1949)	61
R v Collins (1972)	27
R v Deller (1952)	23
R v Donovan (1934)	57
R v Dudley and Stephens (1884)	74
R v Duncalf (1979)	17
R v Dyson (1908)	48
R v Eason (1971)	7
R v Evans (1962)	83
R v Feely (1973)	70
R v Franklin (1883)	81
R v Gibbins and Proctor (1918)	24
R v Gore (1611)	49
R v Gosney (1971)	84

INDEX OF CASES

R v Hamilton (1980)	72
R v Harry (1974)	14
R v Hibbert (1869)	3
R v Howell (1974)	41
R v Hussey (1924)	11
R v Jordan (1956)	51
R v Kemp (1957)	10
R v Lamb (1967)	76
R v Larsonneur (1933)	30
R v Levett (1638)	37
R v Linneker (1906)	32
R v Lipman (1969)	75
R v McCall (1971)	13
R v Martin (1881)	52
R v Miller (1954)	58
R v Mohan (1975)	34
R v O'Brien (1974)	60
R v Paddison (1973)	42
R v Prince (1875)	2
R v Quick (1973)	42
R v Royle (1971)	71
R v Sharp and Johnson (1957)	62
R v Smith (1959)	50
R v Spurge (1961)	77
R v Steane (1947)	68
R v Stephenson (1979)	18
R v Tolson (1889)	9
R v Turner (1971)	78
R v Walkington (1979)	19
R v Warner (1970)	79
R v Williams (1923)	59
R v Willshire (1881)	73
R v Windle (1952)	16
R v Woodman (1974)	26
Read v Coker (1853)	54

S
Shaw v D.P.P. (1961)	29

Sherras v De Rutzen (1895)   20
Sweet v Parsley (1969)   4

T
Thabo Meli v R (1954)   44
Turberville v Savage (1669)   53

W
Woolmington v D.P.P. (1935)   1

CASES

1. Woolmington v Director of Public Prosecutions (1935) – Woolmington was charged with the murder of his wife. He did not deny that he had shot her, but he stated that the gun had gone off accidentally while he was trying to persuade her to return to live with him by threatening to shoot himself. The trial judge in his summing up intimated that once it was proved that Woolmington had shot his wife there was a presumption of murder and the jury accordingly returned a verdict of guilty.

Woolmington appealed against his conviction to the Court of Criminal Appeal, and that court affirmed the conviction and dismissed the appeal on the ground that the direction to the jury had the support of authority.

Woolmington then appealed to the House of Lords which allowed the appeal and quashed the conviction.

Viscount Sankey L.C. stated in his summing up:

"Throughout the tangled web of the English Criminal Law one golden thread is always to be seen, that it is the duty of the prosecution to prove the prisoner's guilt subject to what I have said as to the defence of insanity (McNaghten's case) and subject also to any statutory exception. If, at the end of a whole case, there is reasonable doubt, created by the evidence given by either the prosecution or the prisoner, as to whether the prisoner killed the deceased with a malicious intention, the prosecution has not made out the case and the prisoner is entitled to an acquittal. No matter what the charge or where the trial, the principle that the prosecution must prove the guilt of the prisoner is part of the common law of England and no attempt to whittle it down can be entertained. When dealing with a murder case the Crown must prove (a) death as the result of a voluntary act of the accused and (b) malice of the accused. It may prove malice either expressly or by implication. For malice may be implied where death occurs as the result of a voluntary act of the accused which is (i) intentional and (ii) unprovoked. When evidence of death and malice has been given (a question for the jury) the accused is entitled to show, by evidence or by examination of the circumstances adduced by the Crown that the act on his part which caused death was either unintentional or provoked. If the jury are either satisfied with his explanation or, upon a review of all the evidence, are left in reasonable doubt whether, even if his explanation was not accepted, the act was unintentional or provoked, the prisoner is entitled to be acquitted. It is not the law of England to say, as was said in the summing up in the present case, 'If the Crown satisfy you that this woman died at the prisoner's hands then he has to show that there are circumstances to be found in the evidence which has been given from the witness-box in this case which alleviate the crime so that it is only manslaughter or which excuse the homicide altogether by showing it was a pure accident'."

2. R v Prince (1875) – Prince took an unmarried girl, Annie Phillips, who was under 16, out of the possession and against the will of her father contrary to Section 55 of the Offences Against the Person Act 1861 (now Section 20 of the Sexual Offences Act 1956). The girl looked much older and the jury found that she had told Prince that she was 18, that he in good faith believed her, and that his belief was reasonable. A case was reserved for the Court for Crown Cases Reserved. **Held,** the conviction would be affirmed on the ground that at the time when he took her away Prince knew she was in her father's possession and an honest belief on reasonable grounds that the girl was over 16 years of age was no defence. The legislature had enacted that if anyone did the wrong act he did it at the risk of her turning out to be under 16. The section in question was one of the enactments under the Act forming a code for the protection of women and the guardians of young women and having knowingly done an act, i.e. taking the girl away from the lawful possession of her father against his will and in violation of his rights as guardian by nature, Prince could not say that he thought the girl was of an age beyond that prohibited by the statute.

3. R v Hibbert (1869) – Hibbert met Elizabeth Ann Oldham in the street. He took her to another place where he seduced her and then took her back to the place where he had met her. The girl was 14 years old and Hibbert did not inquire whether she was in the possession of her father or a guardian and did not believe her to be in anyone's care. He was charged with and found guilty of unlawfully taking a girl under 16 out of the possession of and against the will of her father contrary to Section 55 of the Offences against the Person Act 1861 (now Section 20 of the Sexual Offences Act 1956), but a case was reserved for the opinion of the Court for Crown Cases Reserved who quashed the conviction. Bovill C.J. stated "In the present case there is no statement of any finding of fact that the prisoner knew or had reason to believe that the girl was under the lawful care or charge of her father. Still less is there any statement that the prisoner knew that she was under the care of her father as charged in the indictment. In some cases, as, for instance, if the girl were a girl of the town, there would be a probability that the person taking her away had no reason to believe that he was taking her out of the possession of her father or other person. In other cases, again, the surrounding circumstances might be such as to satisfy a jury that he had knowledge that he was taking the girl from the possession of those who lawfully had charge of her. In the absence, however, of any finding of fact on this point the conviction cannot be supported. The decision on which we have arrived is quite in accordance with R v Green where the facts resembled those of the present case. Martin B. there said, 'There must be a taking out of the possession of the father. Here the prisoners picked up the girl in the streets, and for anything that appeared, they might not have known that the girl had a father. The essence of the offence was the taking of the girl out of the possession of the father. The girl was not taken out of the possession of any one. ... The act of the prisoners was scandalous, but it was not any legal offence.' Under these circumstances, therefore, the conviction must be quashed."

4. Sweet v Parsley (1969) – Miss Sweet was the sub-lessee of a farmhouse in the County of Oxford. She sub-let the rooms in the house to various people, retaining one of the rooms for herself, but subsequently moving to another address and only going to the farmhouse in order to collect the rents. Only on very rare occasions did she stay at the farmhouse. Police officers visited the farmhouse one day, and found cigarette ends containing cannabis in the kitchen and boxes of cannabis and LSD hidden in the garden. There was no evidence that Miss Sweet knew that cannabis was being smoked on the premises, nevertheless, she was charged with being concerned in the management of premises used for the purpose of smoking dangerous drugs contrary to Section 5 of the Dangerous Drugs Act 1965.

"If a person (a) being the occupier of premises, permits those premises to be used for the purpose of smoking cannabis or cannabis resin or for dealing in cannabis or cannabis resin, whether by sale, or otherwise or (b) is concerned in the management of any premises used for any such purpose as aforesaid, he shall be guilty of an offence under this Act."

These provisions have been replaced by Section 8 of the Misuse of Drugs Act 1971 which contains the word "knowingly" and makes it clear that mens rea is required.

The magistrates convicted Miss Sweet. Her conviction was affirmed by the Divisional Court and she appealed to the House of Lords.

It was held that the conviction should be quashed.

Lord Pearce stated: "Before the Court will dispense with the necessity for mens rea it has to be satisfied that Parliament so intended. The mere absence of the word 'knowingly' is not enough. But the nature of the crime, the punishment, the absence of social obloquy, the particular mischief and the field of activity in which it occurs, and the wording of the particular section and its context, may show that Parliament intended that the act should be prevented by punishment regardless of intent or knowledge.

Viewing the matter on these principles, it is not possible to accept the respondent's contention. Even granted that this case were in the public health class of case, such as for instance, are offences created to ensure that food shall be clean, it would be quite unreasonable. It is one thing to make a man absolutely responsible for all his own acts and even vicariously liable for his servants if he engages in a certain type of activity. But it is quite another matter to make him liable for persons over whom he has no control. The innocent hotel-keeper, the lady who keeps lodgings or takes paying guests, the manager of a cinema, the warden of a hostel, the matron of a hospital, the housemaster and matron of a boarding school, all these it is conceded, are on the respondent's argument liable to conviction the moment that irresponsible occupants smoke cannabis cigarettes.

If, therefore, the words creating the offence are as wide in their application as the respondent contends, Parliament cannot have intended an offence to which absence of knowledge or mens rea is no defence."

5. Cundy v Le Cocq (1884) – Cundy, a licensed victualler, unknowingly sold liquor to a drunken person, contrary to the Licensing Act 1872 Section 13. The magistrate found that the person to whom the liquor was supplied was drunk, but that Cundy was not aware of this fact and Cundy unsuccessfully appealed to the Divisional Court by way of case stated. Stephen J. in his summing up stated: "I am of the opinion that the words of the section amount to an absolute prohibition of the sale of liquor to a drunken person, and that the existence of a bona fide mistake as to the condition of the person served is not an answer to the charge, but is a matter only for the mitigation of the penalty that may be imposed. I am led to the conclusion both by the general scope of the Act which is for the repression of drunkenness, and from a comparison of the various sections under the head 'offences against public order'. Some of these contain the word 'knowingly', as for instance Section 14 which deals with keeping a disorderly house, and Section 16 which deals with the penalty for harbouring a constable. Knowledge in these and other cases is an element in the offence; but the clause we are considering says nothing about the knowledge of the state of the person served. I believe the reason for making this prohibition absolute was that there must be a great temptation to a publican to sell liquor without regard to the sobriety of the customer and it was thought right to put upon the publican the responsibility of determining whether his customer is sober. Against this view we have had quoted the maxim that in every criminal offence there must be a guilty mind; but I do not think that maxim has so wide an application as it is sometimes considered to have. In old time, and as applicable to the common law or to earlier statutes, the maxim may have been of general application; but a difference has arisen owing to the greater precision of modern statutes. It is impossible now as illustrated by the cases of R v Prince and R v Bishop to apply the maxim generally to all statutes, and the substance of all the reported cases is that it is necessary to look at the object of each Act that is under consideration to see whether and how far knowledge is of the essence of the offence created. Here, as I have already pointed out, the object of this part of the Act is to prevent the sale of intoxicating liquor to drunken persons, and it is perfectly natural to carry that out by throwing on the publican the responsibility of determining whether the person supplied comes within that category.

I think, therefore, the conviction was right and must be affirmed."

6. Haughton v Smith (1973) – A quantity of corned beef was stolen from a firm in Liverpool and some days later an overloaded van travelling south was stopped by the police and the corned beef was found inside. The van was proceeding to a rendezvous with the accused in Hertfordshire where he was to arrange for the disposal of the goods in the London area. Part of the cargo was removed but the van was allowed to proceed with the remainder of the load, two policemen concealed inside and one disguised policeman sitting beside the driver in order to trap the receivers of the goods. When the van arrived at the rendezvous on the M1 at the Scratchwood Service Area in Hertfordshire it was met by Smith and some others by arrangement and then driven to London on Smith's directions but with the police still on board. When the lorry reached its destination, the trap was sprung and various members of the gang arrested. Smith was convicted of attempting to handle stolen goods by dishonestly attempting to assist in the disposal of goods for the benefit of others, knowing or believing the goods to have been stolen. The conviction was quashed by the Court of Appeal and the prosecutor, Mr J. Haughton, Chief Constable of Liverpool, appealed to the House of Lords. The appeal was dismissed as a person can only be convicted of an attempt to commit an offence in circumstances where the steps taken by him in order to commit the offence, if successfully accomplished, would have resulted in the commission of that offence. A person who carried out certain acts in the erroneous belief that those acts constituted an offence could not be convicted of an attempt to commit that offence because he had taken no steps towards the commission of an offence. Also, in order to constitute an offence under Section 22 of the Theft Act 1968 the goods had to be stolen goods at the time of handling, and it was irrelevant that Smith believed them to be stolen goods. Since the goods which Smith had handled were not stolen goods he could not be convicted of attempting to commit the offence.

7. **R v Eason (1971)** − Eason picked up a policewoman's handbag in a cinema, opened it and rustled through the contents. He then replaced the bag, not having taken anything. He was charged with stealing the handbag and its contents and was convicted. He appealed to the Court of Appeal. Per Edmund Davies L.J.:

"In the respectful view of this court, the jury were misdirected. In every case of theft the appropriation must be accompanied by the intention of permanently depriving the owner of his property. What may be loosely described as a 'conditional' appropriation will not do. If the appropriator has it in mind merely to deprive the owner of such of his property as, on examination, proves worth taking and then finding that the booty is to him valueless, leaves it ready to hand to be repossessed by the owner he has not stolen. If a dishonest postal sorter picks up a pile of letters, intending to steal any which are registered, but on finding that none of them are, replaces them, he has stolen nothing, and this is so notwithstanding the provisions of Section 6(1) of the Theft Act 1968. In the present case the jury were never invited to consider the possibility that such was the appellant's state of mind or the legal consequences flowing therefrom. Yet the facts are strongly indicative that this was exactly how his mind was working, for he left the handbag and its contents entirely intact and to hand once he had carried out his exploration. For this reason we hold that conviction of the full offence of theft cannot stand." The appeal was allowed.

8. R v Button (1900) — Button was charged with attempting to obtain money by false pretences. He was a good runner and entered two races at Lincoln in a false name, stating falsely that he had never won a race before and receiving a handicap. He did not claim the money prizes because doubts arose as to his identity and the handicapper asked him if he really was Sims, whether the performance given on the entry form was his and whether he had ever won a race. He answered the questions affirmatively but failed to collect the prizes. In his summing up to the jury, the trial judge directed them to acquit if they were of the opinion that the whole transaction was entered into by the appellant as a joke. The jury returned a verdict of guilty, and a case was reserved for the opinion of the Court for Crown Cases Reserved who held that the appellant had been rightly convicted.

Mathew J. stated: "The questions to be decided in the present case were pure questions of fact, namely, whether the intention of the defendant, when he entered for the races, was to obtain the prizes, and whether he made the representations with that intention. It appears from the case that he pretended to be a man who had never won a foot-race, and he was handicapped on the faith of that statement as is shown by the evidence given by the handicapper; but it also appears from the case that his statement was false, for he had won races. Then it was suggested that he competed in the name of Sims, as is put in the case 'for a lark', but that question was for the jury and they negatived the suggestion. It was also contended that his coming in first in the races was owing to his own good running; but it was also owing, in part at least, to the false pretences, for by means of the false pretences, he obtained a longer start than he would have had if his true name and performances had been known. It is also said that some other act had to be done in order to make the offence complete and that he could not rightly be convicted because it was not shown that he had applied for the prizes, and the criminal intention was exhausted. The argument is exceedingly subtle but unsound. In fact he was found out before he had the opportunity of applying for the prizes as no doubt he otherwise would have done. The pretences which the prisoner made were not too remote, and the conviction was good."

9. R v Tolson (1889) – Mrs Tolson was married to Mr Tolson on 11 September 1880, and was deserted by her husband on 13 December 1881. As a result of enquiries made on her behalf by her father, she was led to believe that her husband had been drowned on his way to America, and on 10 January 1887 she went through a second ceremony of marriage. Mr Tolson returned from America at the end of 1887.

Mrs Tolson was then charged with bigamy contrary to Section 57 of the Offences against the Person Act 1861, under which, "whosoever being married, shall marry any other person during the life of the former husband or wife shall be guilty of felony ... Provided that nothing in this section shall extend to any person marrying a second time whose husband or wife shall have been continually absent from such person for the space of seven years last past and shall not have been known by such person to have been living within that time or shall extend to any person who, at the time of such second marriage, shall have been divorced from the bond of the first marriage, or to any person whose former marriage shall have been declared void by a court of competent jurisdiction."

The jury found as a fact that when she went through the second ceremony she believed in good faith and on reasonable grounds that Tolson was dead. The trial judge directed that this was not a good defence. Upon conviction the case was reserved for the opinion of the Court for Crown Cases Reserved. Nine judges agreed that the conviction was wrong and five judges dissented. At common law an honest and reasonable belief in the existence of circumstances which, if true, would make the act for which the prisoner is indicted an innocent act, is a good defence. Per

Stephen J.: "It could not be the object of Parliament to treat the marriage of widows as an act to be if possible prevented as presumably immoral. The conduct of the woman convicted was not in the smallest degree immoral, it was perfectly natural and legitimate. Assuming the facts to be as she supposed, the infliction of more than a nominal punishment on her would have been a scandal. Why then, should the legislature be held to have wished to subject her to punishment at all?

It is argued that the proviso that a remarriage after seven years' separation shall not be punishable, operates as a tacit exclusion of all other exceptions to the penal part of the section. It appears to me that it only supplies a rule of evidence which is useful in many cases, in the absence of explicit proof of death. But it seems to me to show not that belief in the death of one married person excuses the marriage of the other only after seven years' separation, but that mere separation for that period had the effect which reasonable belief of death caused by other evidence would have at any time. It would to my mind be monstrous to say that seven years' separation should have a greater effect in excusing a bigamous marriage than positive evidence of death, sufficient for the purpose of recovering a policy of assurance or obtaining probate of a will would have, as in the case I put, or in others which might even be stronger." Accordingly, the conviction was quashed.

10. R v Kemp (1957) – Kemp was charged with causing grievous bodily harm to his wife. There was no dispute that he hit her over the head with a hammer without any apparent motive, and that at the time he was unaware of the nature and quality of his act. There was evidence that the accused was suffering from arteriosclerosis which interfered with the flow of blood to his brain. The sole issue was whether the accused was suffering from a disease of the mind in which case the verdict would have been "guilty but insane". Since the Criminal Procedure (Insanity) Act 1964, there would be an acquittal on the ground of insanity. It was held that arteriosclerosis is a disease of the mind within the McNaghten rules and Kemp was insane. Devlin J. stated:

"The law is not in any way concerned with the brain but with the mind in the sense that the term is ordinarily used when speaking of the mental faculties of reasoning, memory and understanding. ... If one read of 'disease of the mind' 'disease of the brain', it would follow that in many cases pleas of insanity would not be established because it would not be established that the brain had been affected by degeneration of the cells or in any other way. In my judgement the condition of the brain is irrelevant and so is the question whether the disease is curable or incurable or whether it is temporary or permanent. There is no warranty for introducing those considerations into the definition of the McNaghten rules. Either temporary or permanent insanity is sufficient to satisfy them.... The hardening of the arteries is a disease which is shown on the evidence to be capable of affecting the mind in such a way as to cause a defect, temporarily or permanent, of its reasoning and understanding and is thus a disease of the mind within the meaning of the rule."

11. R v Hussey (1924) – Hussey's landlady had given him a notice to quit which happened to be invalid. She came with another man forcibly to take the room. Hussey would not retreat or leave, and when the door was being forcibly broken down, he shot through it at the intruder and wounded him. His conviction for malicious wounding was quashed on appeal. Lord Heward said: "In defence of a man's house the owner or his family might kill a trespasser who would forcibly dispossess him of it, in the same manner as he might by law kill in self-defence a man who attacked him personally."

12. Buckoke v Greater London Council (1971) – The Court of Appeal denied that necessity could justify the driver of a fire engine crossing against the lights, even to save life.

13. R v McCall (1971) – McCall told an elderly kind-hearted lady that he had to pay a fine of £310 and that if he did not do so he would be sent to prison. The lady lent him the money and with it McCall bought a car and went to Spain. The Court of Appeal upheld his conviction under Section 15 of the Theft Act.

14. R v Harry (1974) – A student organising a University rag sent letters to shopkeepers telling them that they could avoid "inconvenience" on rag day if they paid up to £5 each into the rag fund. The defendant was charged with blackmail but was acquitted on the direction of the judge, who took the view that the threat was not a menace because it was not likely to affect the mind of an ordinary person.

15. McNaghten's Case (1843) – McNaghten murdered Sir Robert Peel's private secretary and was charged with murder. He pleaded not guilty. Witnesses were called by the defence to prove that the accused was not in a sound state of mind at the time of committing the act. The jury's verdict of "not guilty on the ground of insanity" led to much controversy and finally a debate in the House of Lords, after which the advice of the judges was requested. The judges' reply included the following points:
(1) If the accused did the act complained of knowing at the time he was acting contrary to the law, then notwithstanding a partial delusion regarding his purpose (e.g. acting for the public good) he is nevertheless punishable.
(2) Every man is presumed sane until proved otherwise and to establish a defence on the ground of insanity it must be clearly proved that, at the time of committing the act, the accused was labouring under such a defect of reason, arising from disease of the mind, as not to know the nature and quality of the act he was doing, or, if he did know it, that he did not know he was doing what was wrong.
(3) If a person acts under an insane delusion as to existing facts, then his responsibility must be considered as if the facts of the delusion were real.
(4) A medical expert may only be asked his opinion as to the accused's state of mind at the time of the act if the facts are admitted and the question is purely one of science. He should not be called to give evidence on matters of fact which are for the jury to decide.

16. R v Windle (1952) – The accused admitted giving his wife a fatal dose of aspirin. He had said that he supposed he would hang for it. His defence was insanity. The trial judge refused to leave the question of insanity to the jury and the accused was convicted of murder. He appealed against conviction to the Court of Criminal Appeal. The question to be decided was the meaning of the word "wrong" in the context of the McNaghten Rules and it was held that it meant contrary to law and did not have a vague meaning which might vary according to the opinion of different persons whether a particular act might or might not be justified.

17. R v Duncalf C.A. (G.D.) 1979) – The appellants were convicted of conspiracy to steal, contrary to Sections 1 and 3 of the Criminal Law Act 1977. The facts were that the five appellants had visited 11 shops within 45 minutes, and although they had taken nothing the jury was satisfied that the object of visiting the shops was to see what they could steal. The main ground of appeal was that the appellants had been convicted of an offence which did not exist, and that they should have been charged under Section 5(2) of the 1977 Act which expressly preserves the common law offence of "conspiracy to defraud". Conspiracy to steal, it was argued, must necessarily involve fraud and was therefore outside the scope of statutory conspiracy contrary to Section 1. **Held.** The offence had been correctly charged as contrary to Section 1. The 1977 Act created a new statutory offence of conspiracy which included conspiracy to steal. Conspiracy to defraud remained an offence at common law only in so far as it was necessary to prevent a lacuna being left in the law.

18. R v Stephenson C.A. (G.D.) (1979) – The appellant was convicted of arson contrary to Section 1 of the Criminal Damage Act 1971, having set fire to a large haystack in which he had decided to spend the night. He admitted having started a small fire to keep warm but claimed that the damage was an accident. At his trial medical evidence was called on the appellant's behalf. This showed him to be a schizophrenic which meant that he might not have the same ability to appreciate risk as a normal person. The appellant's conviction rested on the meaning of the word "reckless" within Section 1(1) of the 1971 Act, which the trial judge defined as follows:

"as a man is reckless when he comes out a deliberate act knowing or closing his mind to the obvious fact that there is some risk of damage ... there may be all kinds of reasons which make a man close his mind to the obvious fact; among them may be schizophrenia, that he is a schizophrenic."

An appeal was lodged one of the grounds of which was that this direction failed to make clear to the jury that the test of whether a man was reckless or not was a subjective test. **Held.** The correct test is subjective and not objective. In order to prove that a defendant is reckless the prosecution must show that he carried out a deliberate act of destruction appreciating that there was a risk that damage to property might result from his act. However, not every risk could properly be classed as reckless. The risk must be one which it is in all the circumstances unreasonable for him to take. The appellant's schizophrenia might have prevented him appreciating the risk which would have been obvious to a normal person. Since this was a matter which had not been clearly left to the jury to decide, the conviction was unsafe and must be quashed.

19. R v Walkington (1979) – The accused entered a department store shortly before it was due to close. He made his way to the first floor, entered a three-sided counter area reserved for staff. Once inside he pulled a till drawer open, noticed it was empty and slammed it shut. The accused was convicted of burglary contrary to Section 9(1)(a) of the Theft Act 1968 in that he entered as a trespasser part of a building with intent to steal therein. He appealed against his conviction to the Court of Appeal on the ground, inter alia, that the trial judge should have withdrawn the case from the jury because the counter area could not constitute "part of a building" for the purposes of Section 9. **Held** that it was up to the jury to decide whether the counter area was "part of a building" to which the general public were prohibited entry. Having regard to the facts there was ample evidence of this and also of the fact that the accused knew that the area in question was "off limits".

20. Sherras v De Rutzen (1895) – The appellant, a licensed victualler, was convicted by a magistrate of supplying liquor to a constable on duty without the authority of his superior officer, under the Licensing Act 1872. The appellant's daughter had served the constable in his presence. The constable had removed his armlet which had to be worn when on duty and no question was asked as to whether he was on duty. It was found as a fact by the magistrate that the appellant did not know that the constable was on duty. There was no intention to do a wrongful act. "There is a presumption that mens rea, an evil intention, or a knowledge of the wrongfulness of the act, is an essential ingredient in every offence; but that presumption is liable to be displaced either by the words of the statute creating the offence or by the subject matter with which it deals, and both must be considered ... there must in general be guilty knowledge on the part of the defendant, or of some one whom he has put in his place to act for him, generally or in the particular matter, in order to constitute an offence", per Wright J. The conviction was quashed.

21. Attorney-General for Northern Ireland v Gallagher (1963) – The accused was charged with murdering his wife. He had indicated an intention to kill her and then had bought a knife and a bottle of whisky,

CRIMINAL LAW

which he had drunk before the killing. His defence was insanity under the McNaghten rules or alternatively that he was so drunk at the time of the killing that he was incapable of forming the intent to murder. He was convicted and appealed successfully to the Court of Appeal in Northern Ireland. The prosecution appealed to the House of Lords who allowed the appeal per Lord Denning: "I would agree, of course, that if before the killing he had discarded his intention to kill or reversed it, and then got drunk, it would be a different matter. But when he forms the intention to kill and without interruption proceeds to get drunk and carry out his intention, then his drunkenness is no defence and nonetheless so because it is dressed up as a defence of insanity. There was no evidence in this case of any interruption and there was no need for the Lord Chief Justice to mention it to the jury."

22. Director of Public Prosecutions v Newbury and Jones (1976) – The train travelling from Pontypridd to Cardiff was approaching a bridge which crossed the railway line. The guard was sitting next to the driver of the train in the front cab. The driver noticed the heads of three boys above the parapet of the bridge. He saw one of the boys push something off the parapet towards the train (this proved later to be part of a paving stone). The stone came through the glass window of the cab and killed the guard. The boys were convicted of manslaughter. Their appeal was dismissed by the Court of Appeal and leave was granted to appeal to the House of Lords. The point of law certified to be of general public importance was "Can a defendant be properly convicted of manslaughter, when his mind is not affected by drink or drugs, if he did not foresee that his act might cause harm to another?"

Lord Salmond said that it is plain,
(a) that an accused is guilty of manslaughter if it is proved that he intentionally did an act which was unlawful and dangerous and that act inadvertently caused death and
(b) that it is unnecessary to prove that the accused knew that the act was unlawful or dangerous. This is one of the reasons why cases of manslaughter vary so infinitely in their gravity. They may amount to little more than pure inadvertence and sometimes to little less than murder.

23. R v Deller (1952) – Deller believing his car to be mortgaged represented to X that it was free from incumbrances whereupon X bought it. It turned out that the mortgage document was void so that the car actually was free from incumbrances. D's conviction under the Larceny Act 1916 for obtaining by false pretences was accordingly quashed because there was no actus reus.

24. R v Gibbins and Proctor (1918) − Gibbins was the father of a child. Proctor who lived with Gibbins as his mistress, with Gibbins' concurrence withheld food from the child, intending the child's death or grievous bodily harm. The child died. Gibbins and Proctor were convicted of murder. Both owed a duty to feed the child which both had failed to perform with the intent necessary for murder.

25. Ferguson v Weaving (1951) − A number of people were convicted of consuming intoxicating liquor in an hotel outside permitted hours, contrary to Section 4 of the Licensing Act 1921. The licensee had instructed the three waiters on duty in the concert room to collect glasses containing intoxicating liquor at ten o'clock before collecting empty glasses and to require persons having glasses containing intoxicating liquor either to drink the liquor or give up the glasses. At five minutes before ten o'clock and again at ten o'clock she gave signals to indicate it was closing time and the waiters called "time". Some time after ten o'clock police officers entered the concert room of the hotel and found a number of persons consuming intoxicating drink but the licensee who was in another room at the time did not know of this. She was acquitted and an appeal was made to the Divisional Court. It was held that the acquittal would be upheld on the ground that the knowledge of the waiters could not be imputed to her so as to make her guilty of aiding and abetting. If Parliament had desired to make a licensee guilty of an offence by allowing persons to consume liquor after hours it would have been perfectly easy so to provide in the section. In this case there is no substantive offence in the licensee at all. The substantive offence is committed only by the customers. She can aid and abet the customers if she knows that the customers are committing the offence, but we are not prepared to hold that knowledge can be imputed to her so as to make her, not a principal offender, but an aider and abetter. So to hold would be in our opinion an unwarranted extension of the doctrine of vicarious responsibility in criminal law.

26. R v Woodman (1974) – Woodman was charged with the theft of scrap metal from a disused factory site owned by English China Clays. They had sold the metal to the Bird Group who had removed most of it, leaving behind some metal considered too inaccessible to be worth removing. English China Clays had then erected a barbed-wire fence around the perimeter and had put up notices "Private Property, Keep Out". English China Clays were not aware that there remained any scrap metal on the site. Woodman took a van to the site and removed some of the metal remaining there. The indictment alleged that the scrap metal belonged to English China Clays. Following conviction Woodman appealed to the Court of Appeal where his appeal was dismissed.

27. R v Collins (1972) – Collins had been drinking heavily and desired sexual relations. He passed the complainant's house about 3.30 a.m. and saw a light on in an upstairs room which he knew was the the complainant's bedroom. He fetched a ladder, put it up against the window and climbed up. Seeing a naked girl asleep on the bed, he stripped, climbed over the window-sill and entered the room. At this point the girl awoke and mistakenly believing that Collins was her boyfriend, welcomed him to her bed, where intercourse took place. After a lapse of some time she became suspicious of the length of Collins hair and his mode of love-talk and she switched on the bedroom light. When she saw that it was not her boyfriend she slapped his face, hit him and told him to go. Collins was convicted of burglary in that he had entered a building as a trespasser with intent to commit rape. He appealed to the Court of Appeal. The conviction was quashed since there cannot be a conviction for entering premises as a trespasser within Section 9 of the Theft Act 1968 unless the person entering did so knowing that he was a trespasser and nevertheless deliberately entered or was reckless whether or not he was entering the premises of another without the party's consent. Edmund Davies L.J. in the course of his judgement said:

"According to the learned editors of Archbold (Criminal Pleading, Evidence and Practice, 37th Edn, 1969, p. 572 para 1505) any intentional, negligent or reckless entry into a building will, it would appear, constitute a trespass if the building is in the possession of another person who does not consent to the entry. Nor will it make any difference if the entry was a result of a reasonable mistake on the part of the defendant, so far as trespass is concerned. If that be right, then it would be no defence for this man to say (and even were he believed in saying), 'Well, I honestly thought that this girl was welcoming me into the room and I therefore entered, believing that I had her consent to go in.' If Archbold is right, he would nevertheless be a trespasser, since the apparent consent of the girl was unreal, she being mistaken as to who was at her window. We disagree. We hold that, for the purpose of Section 9 of the Theft Act 1968, a person entering a building is not guilty of trespass if he enters without knowledge that he is trespassing or at least without acting recklessly as to whether or not he is unlawfully entering."

The appeal was allowed on the basis that the jury were never invited to consider the vital question whether Collins did enter the premises as a trespasser, that is to say knowing perfectly well that he had no invitation to enter or reckless of whether or not his entry was with permission.

28. Laurence v Metropolitan Police Commissioner (1971) − Mr Occhi, an Italian student who spoke little English showed Laurence, a taxi driver, a piece of paper with an address written on it. Laurence told him it would be a long and expensive journey although the legal fare was only about fifty pence. When the time came to pay the fare Occhi opened his wallet and gave £1 to Laurence, who then took a further £6 from the wallet. Laurence was charged with stealing the £6. He was convicted and appealed to the Court of Appeal on the ground that he could not be guilty of stealing since Occhi had consented to the £6 being taken. The appeal was dismissed and he then appealed to the House of Lords. **Held** that the appeal would be dismissed as there was a dishonest appropriation of the money with an intention permanently to deprive Mr Occhi of it. The House stated that: (1) on a charge of theft it is not necessary for the prosecution to establish that the appropriation was without the owner's consent; (2) belief, or the absence thereof, that the owner consented to the appropriation is relevant to the issue of dishonesty, not to the question whether or not there has been an appropriation; (3) proof that the owner consented to the appropriation will not suffice to show there was no dishonesty if the owner's consent was given without full knowledge of the circumstances, but it will be sufficient to show that the accused entertained the belief that in giving his consent the owner had full knowledge of the circumstances; (4) theft and obtaining by deception are not mutually exclusive and therefore a conviction for theft may be sustained even though the facts proved would also justify a conviction for obtaining by deception.

CRIMINAL LAW

An extract from the House of Lord's judgement per Viscount Dilhorne is as follows:

"Megaw L.J.'s Appeal Court judgement: 'The offence created by Section 1(1) involved four elements, (i) a dishonest (ii) appropriation (iii) of property belonging to another (iv) with the intention of permanently depriving the owner of it.' I agree. That there was appropriation in this case is clear. Section 3(1) states that any assumption by a person of the rights of an owner amounts to an appropriation. Here, there was clearly such an assumption. That an appropriation was dishonest may be proved in a number of ways. In this case it was not contended that the appellant had not acted dishonestly. Section 2(1) provides, inter alia, that a person's appropriation of property belonging to another is not to be regarded as dishonest if he appropriates the property in the belief that he would have the other's consent if the other knew of the appropriation and the circumstances of it. A fortiori, a person is not to be regarded as acting dishonestly if he appropriates another's property believing that with full knowledge of the circumstances that other person has in fact agreed to the appropriation. The appellant, if he believed that Mr Occhi knowing that £7 was far in excess of the legal fare, had nevertheless agreed to pay him that sum, could not be said to have acted dishonestly in taking it.

When Megaw L.J. said that if there was true consent, the essential element of dishonesty was not established, I understand him to have meant this. Belief or the absence of belief that the owner had with such knowledge consented to the appropriation is relevant to the issue of dishonesty, not to the question whether or not there has been an appropriation. That may occur even though the owner has permitted or consented to the property being taken. So proof that Mr Occhi had consented to the appropriation of £6 from his wallet without agreeing to paying a sum in excess of the legal fare does not suffice to show that there was not dishonesty in this case. There was ample evidence that there was.

I now turn to the third element, 'property belonging to another'. Counsel for the appellant contended that if Mr Occhi consented to the appellant taking the £6, he consented to the property in the money passing from him to the appellant and that the appellant had not, therefore, appropriated property belonging to another. He argued that the old distinction between the offence of false pretences and larceny had been preserved. I am unable to agree with this. The new offence of obtaining property by deception created by Section 15(1) of the Theft Act 1968 also contains the words 'belonging to another'. 'A person who by any deception dishonestly obtains property belonging to another with the intention of permanently depriving the other of it commits the offence.' 'Belonging to another' in Section 1(1) and in Section 15(1) in my view signifies no more than that, at the time of the appropriation or the obtaining, the property belonged to another with the words belonging to another having the extended meaning given by Section 5.

The first question posed in the certificate of appeal was

'Whether Section 1(1) of the Theft Act 1968 is to be construed as though it contained the words "without having the consent of the owner" or words to that effect.'

In my opinion, the answer is clearly No.

The second question was:

'Whether the provisions of Section 15(1) and of Section 1(1) of the Theft Act 1968 are mutually exclusive in the sense that if the facts proved would justify a conviction under Section 15(1) there cannot lawfully be a conviction under Section 1(1) on those facts.'

Again in my opinion, the answer is No. There is nothing in the Act to suggest that they should be regarded as mutually exclusive and it is by no means uncommon for conduct on the part of the accused to render him liable to conviction for more than one offence. Not infrequently there is some overlapping of offences. In some cases the facts may justify a charge under Section 1(1) and also a charge under Section 15(1). On the other hand there are cases which come only within Section 1(1) and some which are only within Section 15(1). If in this case the appellant had been charged under Section 15(1), he would, I expect, have contended that there was no deception, that he had simply appropriated the money and that he ought to have been charged under Section 1(1). In my view, he was rightly charged under that section."

29. Shaw v Director of Public Prosecutions (1961) – The appellant published a booklet containing the names, addresses and telephone numbers of prostitutes offering their services for sexual intercourse and sexual perversions. The appellant's purpose was to assist the prostitutes to obtain customers when they were no longer able to solicit on the street as a result of the Street Offences Act 1959. The prostitutes paid for the advertisements and the appellant derived profit from the publication. He was charged with (1) conspiracy to corrupt public morals; (2) living on the earning of prostitution contrary to Section 30 of the Sexual Offences Act 1956; (3) publishing an obscene article contrary to Section 2 of the Obscene Publications Act 1959. He was convicted and his appeal was dismissed by the Court of Criminal Appeal. The House of Lords held that (1) the appellant was knowingly living in part on the earnings of prostitution, (2) a conspiracy to corrupt public morals was a common law misdemeanour. Viscount Simonds stated that if it were not so then Her Majesty's Courts would strangely have failed in their duty as servants and guardians of the common law. Lord Reid however dissented. It was however agreed by the House of Lords that they had as regards a custodes morum of the people a residual power, where no statute had yet intervened to supercede the common law, to superintend those offences which were prejudicial to the public welfare. Lord Reid expressed doubts. Where Parliament fears to tread it is not for the courts to rush in.

30. R v Larsonneur (1933) – A French woman who went from England to Ireland was arrested by the Irish police and transported in custody back to England. She was delivered to the English police and charged with an offence under the Aliens Order of being an alien who was "found" in the United Kingdom without permission. The police had found her in their own police station but nevertheless the London Sessions sentenced her to imprisonment for three days with a recommendation for deportation, and the conviction and sentence were upheld by the Court of Criminal Appeal.

31. Gardner v Akeroyd (1952) – The Meat (Prices) (Great Britain) Order 1951 made it an offence to sell meat at above fixed prices, or to attempt to do so or to do acts preparatory to doing so. An inspector found parcels of meat in Akeroyd's butcher's shop bearing the names of purchasers and marked with prices exceeding the maximum. The tickets had been prepared and fixed by Akeroyd's assistant, during Akeroyd's absence and without his knowledge. Had the meat been sold, the full offence would have been committed by Akeroyd, for he would have been vicariously responsible for the act of his assistant, and the regulations did not require mens rea. Since the meat had not been sold, Akeroyd was charged with doing an act preparatory to the commission of an offence. It was held that the doctrine of vicarious liability does not apply on a charge of attempt and on a charge of attempt to commit a strict liability offence mens rea must be proved.

32. R v Linneker (1906) – Linneker was indicted under Section 18 of the Offences against the Person Act 1861, for attempting to discharge a loaded revolver at another with intent to do him grievous bodily harm. He had drawn a loaded revolver from his pocket, but his arm had been seized before he could take aim. He was convicted and the conviction was affirmed by the Court for Crown Cases Reserved.

33. Davey v Lee (1968) – The accused were prosecuted in the magistrates' court for an attempt to steal a quantity of metal. One evening a police officer heard a snipping and scrambling sound coming from the compound of the South Western Electricity Board and saw Michael Rigler and another man at the edge of the compound. Their van was later stopped by another police officer and a pair of wire cutters were found in the pocket of the driver's door. The police officer asked the accused to go to the police station and after the van had gone about ten yards, a pair of bolt croppers were thrown into the hedge. Drums of copper, other stores, an office building and a dwelling house were inside the compound which was enclosed by barbed wire and insulated wire fencing as well as a chain link fence: all the fences were found to have been cut. The men were convicted and after an unsuccessful appeal to Quarter Sessions, they appealed to the Divisional Court, contending that the act of cutting through the fences was not sufficiently proximate to stealing metal and even if their actions did constitute an attempt it could not be held beyond reasonable doubt that it was an attempt to commit larceny of the metal as opposed to an attempt to commit some other offence, as the compound contained other stores. The convictions were affirmed on the ground that the act of cutting through the fences was sufficiently proximate to stealing the metal to constitute an attempt and it was to steal the metal that the accused had cut the fences. The following definition was approved by Lord Parker L.J. and Diplock L.J.:

"The actus reus necessary to constitute an attempt is complete if the prisoner does an act which is a step towards the commission of the specific crime, which is immediately and not merely remotely connected with the commission of it, and the doing of which cannot reasonably be regarded as having any other purpose than the commission of a specific crime."

34. R v Mohan (1975) – A uniformed police officer saw the accused driving a motor-car towards him at a speed which he estimated to be in excess of the permitted limit. He signalled the accused to stop and his response was first to slow down, but then to accelerate and drive straight towards the police officer who jumped aside. The accused was convicted of driving a motor vehicle in a manner dangerous to the public and attempting to cause grievous bodily harm to the police officer. In relation to the second offence, the conviction was quashed as the mens rea for an attempt requires "a decision to bring about, in so far as it lies within the accused's power, the commission of the offence which it is alleged the accused attempted to commit." The trial judge's direction to the jury that it had to be proved that the accused must have realised that his conduct was likely to cause bodily harm or that he was reckless as to the causing of bodily harm, but that it was not necessary to prove an actual intention to cause bodily harm was wrong.

35. Johnson v Phillips (1976) – Johnson stopped his car behind an ambulance in a narrow one-way street. A police officer asked him to reverse to the next street because he was obstructing the removal of injured persons and other ambulances were expected. Johnson refused, and was convicted of obstructing the officer in the execution of his duty. The conviction was affirmed on appeal, the court pointing out that it was the officer's duty to protect life and property, and the manoeuvre required was not dangerous, even though it involved a breach of the letter of the law.

36. R v Bourne (1938) – A 14-year-old girl was violently raped and the accused, an eminent surgeon openly performed an abortion on her in a London hospital. He performed the operation without fee after consulting another doctor and with the mother's consent. The opinion of the surgeons was that the continuance of the pregnancy would cause her serious injury and lead to her being a physical wreck for the rest of her life. He was however charged with unlawfully procuring an abortion. The jury were directed that no person ought to be convicted unless they were satisfied that the operation was not done in good faith for the purpose of preserving the life of the mother. Magnaghten J. continued: "For the preservation of the life of the mother. I do not think that it is contended that these words mean merely for the preservation of the life of the mother from instant death ... if the doctor is of the opinion, on reasonable grounds and with adequate knowledge, that the probable consequence of the continuance of the pregnancy will be to make the woman a physical or mental wreck, the jury are quite entitled to take the view that the doctor who, in these circumstances, and that honest belief operates, is operating for the purpose of preserving the life of the woman." The accused was found not guilty. Such events today would of course be covered by the Abortion Act 1967.

37. R v Levett (1638) – Levett, under the impression that thieves were in the house, stabbed Frances Freeman who had unknown to him been let into the house by his servant believing that she was one of the thieves. He was charged with unlawful homicide but it was resolved that it was not manslaughter for he did the act ignorantly, without intention of hurt to the said Frances.

38. R v Bailey (1800) – On 27 June 1799, Bailey, a ship's captain, without justification fired on another ship on the high seas wounding a sailor and was charged under a statute prohibiting this conduct which was passed on 10 May 1799. Lord Eldon told the jury that he was of the opinion that Bailey was in strict law guilty within the statutes, taken together, if the facts laid were proved, though he could not then know that the Act of 39 George III, c. 37 had passed, and that his ignorance of that fact could in no other wise affect the case, than that it might be the means of recommending him to a merciful consideration elsewhere should he be found guilty. Bailey was convicted even though he could not have known on 27 June 1799 that the relevant statute had been passed. At the following Admiralty Sessions however Bailey was pardoned.

39. Director of Public Prosecutions v Morgan (1975) – Morgan, a senior RAF non-commissioned officer invited three other air force men to have intercourse with his wife. Morgan assured the men that his wife was "kinky" and although she might appear to resist, such resistance was merely simulated. The three men accepted the invitation and despite Mrs Morgan's violent screams and shouts of "Police" they took it in turns to have intercourse. They were convicted of rape after the judge had directed the jury that if they were satisfied that the wife had not given her consent, the belief of the defendants that she had consented was not a defence unless based on reasonable grounds. Their appeals were dismissed by the Court of Appeal. The House of Lords held that the trial judge's summing up was wrong, but no reasonable jury could have failed to convict the appellants even if properly directed; there was no miscarriage of justice and the appeals should be dismissed.

40. Director of Public Prosecutions v Beard (1920) – The appellant raped a girl of 13 and when she struggled he placed his hand upon her mouth and his thumb on her throat and caused her death by suffocation. He pleaded drunkenness as a defence. He was convicted of murder and the Court of Criminal Appeal substituted a verdict of manslaughter upon the ground that the judge was wrong in applying to a case of drunkenness the test of insanity and that he ought to have directed the jury in accordance with the rule laid down in R v Meade, that is they should have been told to acquit unless they were satisfied that the appellant was capable of knowing what he was doing was dangerous. However, the House of Lords restored the conviction as Beard had not been so drunk as to be incapable of forming the intention to have sexual intercourse with the girl without her consent. Lord Birkenhead, delivering the judgement of the court, stated that (a) evidence of drunkenness which rendered the accused incapable of forming the specific intent essential to constitute the crime ought to be taken into account with the other facts proved, in order to determine whether he had that intent; (b) the test of criminal responsibility is not the same in the case of drunkenness as in the case of insanity, and upon a plea of drunkenness where insanity is not pleaded, the jury should not be asked to consider whether, if the accused knew what he was doing, he knew also that he was doing wrong.

41. R v Howell (1974) – The accused was charged with the murder of Linda Thomas, a taxi driver, whose body was found in an old mine. He said he could remember the physical blows he rained on her but could not explain why he had acted in such a way. He had no intention of harming her and no control over his actions. Following Gray v Barr (1971) and R v Lipman (1969), the judge was invited to direct the jury that if they found that the degree of intoxication by the defendant was so great as to render him incapable of having any intention to cause harm to the dead girl then they would be entitled to acquit him. Mr Justice Wien stated in his judgement that he proposed to direct the jury that self-induced intoxication resulting from drink or drugs or both is no defence to manslaughter however great the degree of intoxication. If the defendant's acts were likely to cause harm to Linda Thomas then an acquittal was impossible and at the very least there must be a verdict of guilty of manslaughter. In fact the defendant was found guilty of murder.

42. R v Quick and R v Paddison (1973) – The defendants, Quick, a charge nurse and Paddison, a state-enrolled nurse, were employed at a mental hospital. They were charged with assaulting a patient and causing grievous bodily harm. They pleaded not guilty. Quick, a diabetic, raised the defence of automatism. He said that he had taken insulin, as prescribed, on the morning of the assault, had drunk spirits, and eaten little food, and could not remember the assault. Medical evidence suggested that at the material time his condition was consistent with a hypoglycaemic state. The judge ruled that the evidence could only support a defence of insanity, not automatism. Quick then pleaded guilty, and Paddison was convicted of aiding and abetting by encouragement. They were convicted and appealed to the Court of Appeal which quashed the convictions and held that in respect of Quick, (1) In order to sustain a defence of insanity on the ground that he was suffering from a deflect of reason from disease of the mind he would have to show a malfunctioning of the mind caused by disease: a malfunctioning of the mind of transitory effect caused by the application to the body of some external factor, such as violence, drugs, including anaesthetics, alcohol and hypnotic influences, could not be said to be due to disease; (2) The mental condition from which he had been suffering had not been caused by his diabetes but by the use of insulin prescribed by his doctor; the alleged malfunctioning of his mind had therefore been caused by an external factor and not by a bodily disorder in the nature of a disease and he was entitled to have his defences of automatism left to the jury.

43. Hill v Baxter (1958) – Baxter was charged with dangerous driving and failing to stop at a "Halt" sign. He pleaded that he remembered nothing after the accident which occurred. The magistrates dismissed the information. On appeal it was held that mens rea was no part of the offences. There was no evidence to justify the finding that the driver was not fully responsible in law for his actions, and the case would be remitted to the magistrates with a direction to convict.

44. Thabo Meli v R (1954) – Four men were charged with murder. They had connived to kill the deceased and then make out that he died in an accident. Thabo Meli invited the deceased to a hut, gave him beer and when he became rather merry hit him on the head. Believing him to be dead, he then rolled the body over a cliff and made it appear that he had suffered an accident. The medical evidence showed that the deceased did not die from the blow he received but from exposure at the foot of the cliff. The men were convicted and ultimately appealed to the Judicial Committee of the Privy Council raising as a defence that there were two separate acts; the attack in the hut which although accompanied by mens rea did not cause death, and the rolling of the body over the cliff which although it caused death was not accompanied by mens rea. The conviction was affirmed on the ground that the whole affair was one single transaction and could not be divided in the way suggested.

45. R v Church (1966) – Church was charged with the murder of a woman. He had taken her in a van near a river in order to have sexual intercourse. He had been unable to satisfy her whereupon she taunted him and he had fought with her knocking her unconscious. He tried for about half an hour to revive her but then panicked and threw her body into the river. The woman was not dead when she was thrown into the river but continued to breathe for some time and eventually died from drowning. He was acquitted of murder, but convicted of manslaughter and appealed to the Court of Criminal Appeal. The Court affirmed the conviction on the ground that he was guilty of criminal negligence by not endeavouring to ascertain whether or not the woman was still alive when he threw the body into the river and that the woman died as a result of an unlawful act which a reasonable man would regard as likely to cause harm. The Court also stated that the jury could have convicted on murder, even though Church thought his blows and attempted strangulation had actually produced death when he threw the body into the river; if they regarded his behaviour from the moment he first struck her to the moment when he threw the body into the river as a series of acts designed to cause death or grievous bodily harm.

46. Hyam v Director of Public Prosecutions (1974) – Mrs Hyam had an affair with Mr Jones which ended when he became engaged to Mrs Booth. Mrs Hyam therefore on 15 July 1972 poured half a gallon of petrol through Mrs Booth's letter box in the small hours of the morning and set it alight by means of a newspaper and a match. Mrs Booth's two daughters died in the ensuing fire. She was charged with murder and her defence was that she had only started the fire to frighten Mrs Booth into leaving the district. The judge directed the jury that "The prosecution must prove, beyond all reasonable doubt, that the accused intended to kill or do serious bodily harm to Mrs Booth, the mother of the deceased girls. If you are satisfied that when the accused set fire to the house she knew that it was highly probable that this would cause death or serious bodily harm then the prosecution will have established the necessary intent. It matters not if her motive was, as she says, to frighten Mrs Booth." The House of Lords upheld the decision, Lord Diplock saying, "In crimes of this class no distinction is to be drawn in English law between the state of mind of one who does an act because he desires it to produce a particular evil consequence, and the state of mind of one who does the act knowing full well that it is likely to produce that consequence although it may not be the object he was seeking to achieve by doing that act. What is common to both these states of mind is willingness to produce the particular evil consequence and this is the mens rea needed to satisfy a requirement that he must have acted with 'intent' to produce a particular evil consequence."

47. Director of Public Prosecutions v Smith (1961) − A car driven by Smith, containing stolen goods, was stopped by P.C. Meehan, who was on point duty. Smith was questioned about the contents of the car and was asked to pull into the kerb. However, he accelerated with the constable clinging to the side of the car. Meehan was thrown off the car and was killed by an oncoming vehicle. Smith was convicted of capital murder, the jury having been directed that if they were satisfied that Smith, as a reasonable man, must have contemplated that grievous bodily harm was likely to result to Meehan, and that such harm did occur, and Meehan died in consequence, then Smith was guilty of capital murder. The Court of Criminal Appeal substituted a conviction of manslaughter. The Crown appealed to the House of Lords which allowed the appeal and the conviction of murder was restored. It was held that the jury must be satisfied that the accused was unlawfully and voluntarily doing an act aimed at someone, and it is immaterial what in fact he contemplated as the probable result of his action or whether he contemplated it at all. Provided he was in law responsible and accountable for his actions, i.e. capable of forming an intent, not insane nor suffering diminished responsibility, the sole question was whether the unlawful and voluntary act was of such a kind that grievous bodily harm was the natural and probable result. The test was whether the ordinary reasonable man would have contemplated that the unlawful and voluntary act would lead to such a result. The true question in each case is whether there is a real probability of grievous bodily harm. The expression "grievous bodily harm" should bear its ordinary and natural meaning of "really serious" harm.

48. R v Dyson (1908) – The accused, in November 1906, seized his three months' old child by the legs, flung him down and beat him until he became unconscious and his skull had been fractured. On 29 December 1907, he beat the child again bruising it severely about the head and face. On 17 February 1908, at which time the bruises inflicted in 1907 had disappeared, the child was admitted to hospital suffering from traumatic meningitis. It died in March 1908. The accused was found guilty of manslaughter and appealed against conviction to the Court of Criminal Appeal. It was held that the conviction should be quashed on the ground that no person can be convicted of murder unless the death occurred within a year and a day after the injury was inflicted and therefore the judge's summing-up amounted to a misdirection.

49. R v Gore (1611) – Agnes Gore mixed ratsbone with her husband's medicine. He took it, and, his condition suddenly worsening, the medicine was suspected. The apothecary who had prepared it, to prove there was nothing wrong with it, swallowed some of it himself and soon after died. Agnes was convicted of the murder of the apothecary, because "the law conjoins the murderous intention with the event which thence ensued".

50. R v Smith (1959) – Smith stabbed Private Creed in a fight at their barracks. The man's lung was pierced and he was taken to the medical reception station. Another soldier tried to carry Creed to the Medical station but dropped him twice on the way. On his arrival it was not realised how seriously ill he was and he received treatment which was not only inappropriate but positively harmful and he died a couple of hours later. Smith was convicted of murder and The Courts Martial Appeal Court dismissed the appeal. Lord Parker C.J. stated:

"It seems to the court that, if at the time of death the original wound is still an operating cause and a substantial cause, then the death can properly be said to be the result of the wound, albeit that some other cause of death is also operating. Only if it can be said the original wounding is merely the setting in which another cause operates can it be said that the death does not result from the wound. Putting it another way, only if the second cause is so overwhelming as to make the original wound merely part of the history can it be said that the death does not follow from the wound."

51. R v Jordan (1956) – The defendant stabbed a man in a café. The man later died and James Jordan was charged with his murder. However, fresh medical evidence came before the Court of Appeal that death had not in fact been caused by the stab wound but rather by the treatment with terramycin, an antibiotic drug to which the deceased was intolerant, and by the intravenous introduction of abnormal quantities of liquid, so that death resulted from broncho-pneumonia. The Court of Appeal quashed the conviction because of the improper medical treatment. Hallet J. said:

"It is sufficient to point out here that this was not normal treatment. Not only one feature, but two separate and independent features of treatment were, in the opinion of the doctors, palpably wrong and these produced the symptoms discovered at the post-mortem examination which were the direct and immediate cause of death, namely the pneumonia resulting from the condition of oedema which was found."

52. R v Martin (1881) – Shortly before the end of a performance in a theatre, the accused who intended to cause terror in the minds of the audience, turned off the lights on a staircase and placed an iron bar across one of the doorways. In the ensuing panic several persons suffered injury. The accused was charged with inflicting grievous bodily harm, contrary to the Offences against the Person Act 1861 Section 20. He was convicted and a case was stated for the opinion of the Court for Crown Cases Reserved. The court affirmed the conviction, Lord Coleridge C.J. stating: "The prisoner must be taken to have intended the natural consequences of that which he did. He acted 'unlawfully and maliciously', not that he had any personal malice against the particular individuals injured but in the sense of doing an unlawful act calculated to injure, and by which others were in fact injured. Just as in the case of a man who unlawfully fires a gun among a crowd, it is murder if one of the crowd is thereby killed. The prisoner was most properly convicted."

53. Turberville v Savage (1669) – Turberville and Savage were quarrelling. Turberville laid his hand on his sword and said to Savage: "If it were not assize-time, I would not take such language from you." These words negatived any threat, but nevertheless Savage thrust at Turberville and put out his eye. Turberville sued for damages for assault: Savage pleaded self-defence because he feared an attack. It was held that Turberville had not opened the hostilities, because his words showed no present intention to do violence. Consequently Savage was not entitled to claim that he acted in self-defence.

54. Read v Coker (1853) – The defendant collected some men who mustered round the plaintiff, tucked up their sleeves and threatened to break his neck if he did not leave the premises. Plaintiff left and successfully sued the defendant for assault. In essence the assault was by words but there was some threatening conduct by the defendant and his men for they tucked up their sleeves.

55. Fagan v Metropolitan Police Commissioner (1968) – Fagan was driving his car when he was told by a constable to draw into the kerb. He stopped his car with one wheel on the constable's foot and refused to remove it when asked several times to do so. Eventually he relented and moved the car. He was convicted of assault on the constable and Quarter Sessions dismissed his appeal. He then appealed to the Queen's Bench Divisional Court where it was held, dismissing the appeal, that whether or not the mounting of the wheel on the constable's foot had been intentional the defendant had deliberately allowed it to remain there when asked to move it and that constituted an assault. The reasons given by James J. were not however particularly convincing:

"In our judgement the Willesden magistrates and quarter sessions were right in law. On the facts found the action of the apellant may have been initially unintentional, but the time came when, knowing that the wheel was on the officer's foot, the appellant:
(1) remained seated in the car so that his body through the medium of the car was in contact with the officer;
(2) switched off the ignition of the car;
(3) maintained the wheel of the car on the foot;
(4) used words indicating the intention of keeping the wheel in that position.

There was an act constituting battery which at its inception was not criminal because there was no element of intention but which became criminal from the moment the intention was formed to produce the apprehension which was flowing from the continuing act."

It would appear that if Fagan had left the car on the constable's foot and strolled down the road he would not have been guilty of assault, but possibly of false imprisonment.

56. Coward v Baddeley (1859) – A saw a house on fire and advised B, a fireman, to play his hose on the adjoining building, and A touched B in the course of this. B claimed that he had been assaulted, and had A taken into police custody.

It was held that A had touched B merely to attract his attention and this was not assault.

57. R v Donovan (1934) – Donovan made several telephone calls to a 17-year-old girl in which he said he wanted to beat her. The girl consented to be beaten by Donovan. Accordingly the parties met at Marble Arch and Donovan asked her whether she would like to be spanked in Hyde Park or in his garage. They went to the garage where he beat her. He was convicted of indecent and common assault. The Court of Criminal Appeal held that the conviction should be quashed as the trial judge had misdirected the jury on the question of consent and the onus of proof. The court stated that consent is no defence where an act is unlawful in the sense of being a criminal act, and it is unlawful to beat another person with such a degree of violence that the infliction of bodily harm is a probable consequence. There are however many gradations between a slight tap and a severe blow and the question whether particular blows were likely or intended to cause bodily harm is one eminently fitted for the decision of a jury upon evidence which they have heard. The Court had little doubt what the decision would have been but they could not, consistently with the practice of the Court, substitute themselves for the jury and decide a question of fact which was never left to them. It was impossible to say that the appellant's act was unlawful in itself and without such proof he could only be convicted if the prosecution negatived consent.

58. R v Miller (1954) – The husband was charged with rape and assault occasioning bodily harm against his wife who had left him and filed a petition for divorce on the ground of adultery. The hearing of the petition started and was adjourned so that the accused might attend and give evidence. It was after the adjournment that the accused had intercourse with his wife against her will. He was alleged to have used force against her and afterwards she was in a hysterical and nervous condition. It was held that separation and the presentation of a petition for divorce did not amount to a revocation of consent to marital intercourse impliedly given on marriage. The implied consent had not been revoked by any act of the parties or by an order or decree of the Court. The husband could not therefore be guilty of rape, although he was guilty of assault for using violence to exercise his right of marital intercourse.

59. R v Williams (1923) – Williams, a singing teacher was charged with rape. With the consent of her parents he began to give lessons in singing and voice production to a 16-year-old girl. One day he told her she was not producing her notes properly and that she should lay down on the settee. He then removed some of her clothing, placed an instrument on the lower part of her body, and finally had sexual intercourse with her saying that it was a method of making an air passage and improving her voice. The girl believed him and offered no resistance not appreciating the fact that sexual intercourse was taking place. Williams was convicted and appealed to the Court of Criminal Appeal which affirmed the conviction on the ground that a consent obtained by fraud as to the nature of the act is no defence to a prosecution for rape.

60. R v O'Brien (1974) – O'Brien was charged on indictment with raping Christine, who, until 10 January 1974, when she was granted a decree nisi, was his wife. The raping took place on the 12 January 1974. O'Brien moved to quash the indictment on the ground that, as Christine was his wife until the decree absolute was pronounced no offence had been committed. It was held that a decree nisi effectively terminated a marriage and thereupon the consent to marital intercourse impliedly given by a wife at the time of the marriage was revoked. It followed the accused had committed the offence of rape if he had sexual intercourse with Christine after 10 January 1974 without her consent.

61. R v Clarke (1949) – Clarke was charged with the rape of his wife. The parties were married in 1938 and in 1949 the wife obtained a separation order from the justices on the ground of Clarke's persistent cruelty. The separation order contained a provision that the wife should no longer be bound to cohabit with him and although it could be discharged if she committed adultery or if she voluntarily resumed cohabitation with Clarke, it was still in force at the time the offence was committed. The trial judge rejected a motion to quash the indictment on the ground that although as a general rule a husband cannot be guilty of a rape on his wife, since by virtue of the marriage she is deemed to consent to intercourse, her consent to intercourse was revoked by the separation order so that Clarke was not entitled to have intercourse with her without her consent. Clarke was therefore convicted.

62. R v Sharp and Johnson (1957) – A police officer saw Sharp and Johnson fighting in the street in the presence of a large crowd. Their faces and clothing were covered in blood and they were seriously wounded. They were convicted of making an affray and appealed to the Court of Criminal Appeal contending that there could not be an affray unless someone was actually frightened. It was held that the convictions would be quashed because of a misdirection by the trial judge, but the Court stated that an affray can be committed even though no person is actually called to say that he was put in terror.

63. Duncan v Jones (1936) – Mrs Duncan, a woman speaker, was forbidden on her arrival by Mr Jones, a police officer, to hold a meeting at a place opposite a training centre for the unemployed. Fourteen months previously Mrs Duncan had held a meeting at the same spot which had been followed by a disturbance in the centre attributed to the meeting. Mrs Duncan mounted a box to start the meeting but was taken into custody and charged under the Prevention of Crimes Act 1871 and 1885, with obstructing a police officer in the execution of his duty. There was no allegation of obstruction of the highway or of inciting or provoking any person to commit a breach of the peace. Quarter Sessions found (a) that Mrs Duncan must have known of the probable consequences of her holding the meeting, namely a disturbance, and possibly a breach of the peace, and was not unwilling that such consequences should ensue; (b) that Jones reasonably apprehended a breach of the peace; (c) that in law it therefore became his duty to prevent the holding of the meeting; (d) that by attempting to hold the meeting Mrs Duncan obstructed Jones when in the execution of his duty. On appeal to the Divisional Court it was held that Mrs Duncan had been rightly convicted.

64. R v Bogacki (1973) – Three men went to a bus garage after celebrating at a New Year party. They tried to obtain change in order to buy cigarettes from a vending machine, but their request was refused and they were told to go away. On their way out of the garage they boarded a single decker bus which was standing on the forecourt and Stephen Bogacki turned the engine over with the starter as if to start it. The bus never moved and the men got off and went to a nearby police station where they succeeded in obtaining change. Shortly after they were arrested and were later convicted of attempting to take a motor-vehicle without authority, contrary to the Theft Act 1968. They appealed. The Court of Appeal quashed their convictions on the grounds of a misdirection in the summing up of the trial judge with regard to the word "take" which he said suggested the acquisition of possession. The Court of Appeal stated that the word "take" was equivalent to "use" and should be given its ordinary and natural meaning and mere unauthorised use of itself constitutes an offence under Section 12 of the Theft Act. It was further held that before there can be a conviction for the complete offence it must be shown that he took the vehicle, that is that there was an unauthorised taking possession or control of the vehicle by him adverse to the rights of the true owner or person otherwise entitled to such possession or control, coupled with some movement, however small of that vehicle following such unauthorised taking.

65. Atwal v Massey (1971) – This was an appeal by way of case stated against a conviction by the justices for receiving stolen goods contrary to Section 22 of the Theft Act 1968. A thief had left a stolen electric kettle by the roadside for collection by the appellant who had paid him the sum of £1.50. The magistrates clearly took the view that the defendant ought to have known from the unusual circumstances that the kettle had been stolen. The Divisional Court quashed the conviction because the magistrates had incorrectly applied an objective test, for in the words of the Lord Chief Justice:

"If when the justices say that the appellant ought to have known that the kettle was stolen they mean that any reasonable man would have realised that it was stolen then this is not the right test. It is not sufficient to establish an offence under Section 22 that the goods were received in circumstances which would have placed a reasonable man on his inquiry. The question is a subjective one: was the appellant aware of the theft or did he believe the goods to be stolen or did he, suspecting the goods to be stolen, deliberately shut his eyes to the consequences?"

66. Joyce v Director of Public Prosecutions (1946) – Joyce was born in the United States, the son of a naturalised American citizen born in Britain. Joyce was educated to a large extent in England and by falsely representing that he was a British subject he obtained a British passport. He went abroad in 1939 and during the war he broadcast anti-British propaganda from Germany and owing to the general tone of his voice and the inflexion used in his call-sign, "Germany calling", he became known as Lord Haw-Haw. He was convicted of one count of treason, namely adhering to the King's enemies elsewhere than in the King's Realm. Joyce appealed to the Court of Criminal Appeal and to the House of Lords contending that he could not be guilty of treason as he owed no allegiance to the Crown. The House of Lords held that the possession of a British passport enables an alien to obtain in a foreign country the protection entitled to British subjects and consequently such an alien owes a corresponding duty of allegiance.

67. R v Casement (1917) – During the war between Britain and Germany the appellant, who was a British subject, with intent to do so gave aid and comfort to an enemy by means of soliciting and persuading a number of prisoners of war in Germany to foresake their duties and allegiance to the King and join the armed forces of Germany and fight against the King. During January and February 1915, he circulated a leaflet to a number of British prisoners of war advising them to no longer fight for Britain but to join an Irish Brigade that was being formed and equipped by the German government to fight for Ireland.

In 1916 Casement left Germany with an armed expedition force equipped by the German government with the intent of landing arms and ammunition on the coast of Ireland to be used by the Germans in waging war against Britain. He was convicted of high treason and appealed to the Court of Criminal Appeal. It was held that the conviction would be affirmed on the ground that an offence under the 1351 Act is committed where a British subject adheres to the King's enemies by giving them aid and comfort whether within the realm or elsewhere.

68. R v Steane (1947) – Steane was charged under the Defence (General) Regulations 1939 with "doing acts likely to assist the enemy, with intent to assist the enemy". He had been employed as a film actor in Germany for some time before the outbreak of the war of 1939–45, and he was then residing in Germany with his wife and children.

Shortly after the outbreak of the war, he had an interview with German government officials at which he was roughly treated and told to say "Heil Hitler!" In consequence of threats subsequently made against himself, his wife and children, he broadcast news for the Germans between January and April 1940. Subsequently, and after further threats were made against himself and his family, he returned to work for his former employer and helped with the preparation of films until 1945.

He maintained that throughout the period he had no intention or idea of assisting the enemy, and that his sole object had been to save his wife and children from trouble.

The judge directed the jury that, if they were satisfied that the accused had done acts which were likely to assist the enemy, the intent to do so might be presumed and Steane was convicted.

He appealed to the Court of Criminal Appeal against his conviction which was quashed on the ground of misdirection of the jury.

69. Abbot v R (1976) – Abbot was a member of a commune which occupied a house in Trinidad. The commune was presided over by a man called Malik whom Abbot had reason to regard as a dangerous man. On the directions of Malik, Abbot, with others, brutally killed a young woman who was the mistress of a member of the commune. Abbot took an active and prominent part in the killing of the young woman, Gale Benson, by holding her while others tried to kill her with a cutlass and together with three other men burying her dying body. At his trial for murder Abbot claimed that he had acted as he had done because Malik had threatened to kill him and his mother unless his instructions were obeyed. Abbot was convicted of murder and appealed on the ground that the trial judge had failed to direct the jury to consider whether, on the evidence, he was entitled to be acquitted on the ground that he had acted under duress. The Court of Appeal of Trinidad and Tobago dismissed Abbott's appeal and he appealed to the Privy Council. It was held by a majority that the defence of duress was not in law available to a person charged with murder as a principal in the first degree. Their Lordships declined to extend the decision reached in Lynch v Director of Public Prosecutions in Northern Ireland where duress was accepted as a complete defence to anyone charged with murder as a principal in the second degree. To accept that defence in this case might well have far-reaching and disastrous consequences for public safety to say nothing of its important social, ethical and maybe political implications. In a dissenting judgement, Lord Wilberforce and Lord Edmund-Davies said that the evidence as to duress was of such a nature that the interests of justice demanded that a new trial be ordered in order that the evidence should be given consideration. "To hold that a principal in the first degree in murder is never in any circumstances to be entitled to plead duress whereas a principal in the second degree may, is to import the possibility of grave injustice into the common law. Such a conclusion should not be arrived at unless supported by compelling authority or by the demands of public policy shown to operate differently in the two cases. There are no authorities compelling this Court so to hold, nor are there reasons of public policy present in this case which are lacking in the case of principals in the second degree." The appeal was dismissed.

70. R v Feely (1973) – Feely was a branch manager of a firm of bookmakers who, like other employees of the firm, had received a circular from his employers forbidding him to borrow their money by taking it from the till. He took about £30 from a safe at his branch and when the deficiency was discovered he gave an IOU to his successor as branch manager and said that he intended to repay the sum, taking it out of money due from his employers, who owed him about twice that amount.

Feely was charged with theft and convicted after the judge had directed the jury that it is dishonest for an employee to do what he knows his employers are not prepared to tolerate, but had failed to make it plain to the jury that it was for them to decide whether the accused's conduct was in fact dishonest. Feely successfully appealed to the Court of Appeal who quashed his conviction on the ground that the question of whether an appropriation was dishonest was one of fact.

Lawton L.J. said: "In Section 1(1) of the Theft Act 1968 the word 'dishonestly' can only relate to the state of mind of the person who does the act which amounts to appropriation whether an accused person has a particular state of mind as a question of fact which has to be decided by the jury when there is a trial on indictment and by the justices when there are summary proceedings. The Crown did not dispute this proposition, but it was submitted that in some cases (and this, it was said, was such a one) it was necessary for the trial judge to define 'dishonestly' and when the facts fell within the definition he had a duty to tell the jury that if there had been an appropriation it must have been dishonestly done. We do not agree that judges should define what 'dishonestly' means, the word is commonly used. ... The meaning of an ordinary word of the English language is not a question of law. The proper construction of a statute is a question of law. If the context shows that a word is used in an unusual sense the court will determine in other words what the unusual sense is."

71. R v Royle (1971) – Royle was convicted on four counts of obtaining property by deception and on three counts of obtaining a pecuniary advantage by deception. He appealed against his conviction relating to the obtaining pecuniary advantages and against sentence on all counts. Royle was financial adviser to Whitcroft Finance Ltd and had to travel to interview prospective agents for the company. The accounts relating to the use of the hotels were sent to the company and remained unpaid for several months. Eventually cheques drawn by another company for the full amounts were sent to the hotels concerned. It appeared that Royle had evaded a debt by deception in that he had made false representations that his company was carrying on a genuine business and that they intended to pay for accommodation services on presentation of the account. The appeal was allowed and the convictions quashed because:

(a) The jury should have been directed that on the question of dishonesty the test was whether the accused had an honest belief and that, whereas the absence of reasonable ground for the belief that the hotel bills would be met by Whitcroft Finance Ltd might point strongly to the conclusion that he entertained no genuine belief in the truth of his representations, it was for them to say whether or not it had been established that Royle had no such genuine belief.

(b) The jury had not been directed that, before Royle could be said to have evaded a debt, it had to be established that a debt had been incurred which Royle had made himself liable to pay or for which he was or might become liable; there was some evidence which, properly examined, might have led the jury to conclude that the incurring by the appellant of personal liability had not been established.

(c) The direction that it was irrelevant that the debts might be discharged in the future meant that the element of evasion of the debts was never properly explored: the question of whether the debts might be discharged could have some bearing on the essential elements of deception and dishonesty and could support an argument that the debts had been "deferred" rather than evaded.

(d) It was incumbent on the Crown to establish that it was by means of the alleged deception that the appellant obtained "pecuniary advantage" from the hotels concerned. This matter was nowhere dealt with by the commissioner who heard the trial at first instance yet it was basic to the charge. Instead, the commissioner took for granted the nexus between the making of representations to the hotel managements and the fact that thereafter Edmund Davies L.J. stated "That this will not do is amply demonstrated by the concession made by counsel for the Crown before us that he cannot support the conviction on count 7 because the evidence showed that credit was granted because the Midland Hotel manager trusted the appellant as an old customer and in no way because of what he said or because of the contents of the letter which arrived during his stay there. Other criticisms of the summing up could be advanced, but we have said sufficient to indicate why in our view the conviction on these three hotel counts cannot stand. It follows that the appeal must be allowed and the convictions quashed."

72. R v Hamilton (1980) – Lord Lane, Lord Chief Justice, sitting in the Court of Appeal said that is was not only misleading but wrong to invite a jury to judge between grievous bodily harm and actual bodily harm by assessing the degree of seriousness of an assault. One had only to consider the proposition to realise the fallacy it contained. One could, and frequently did, have a very serious assault, e.g. by a knife or a gun, the knife thrust being parried or the gun having been wrongly aimed, which resulted in no injury.

The Court quashed the conviction of the appellant by the Inner London Crown Court for inflicting grievous bodily harm on a neighbour, on an indictment containing an alternative count of assault occasioning actual bodily harm. He received a nine month's sentence. The Lord Chief Justice said that, unhappily, there was a total absence in the summing up of a direction on self-defence, which was the appellant's defence.

73. R v Willshire (1881) – The accused was already convicted of a previous marriage to one Charlotte. He married again whilst Charlotte was still alive. The prosecution's attempt to secure a conviction failed because the marriage to Charlotte on which the prosecution relied in the indictment was invalid so that the prosecution had failed to establish that the previous marriage had been both validly contracted and was subsisting at the time of the ceremony. Willshire had not married Edith Miller while his wife Charlotte was still alive because Charlotte had never been his wife. He was therefore not guilty.

74. R v Dudley and Stephens (1884) – Dudley and Stephens, the deceased and a fourth person were adrift in an open boat a thousand miles from land. After a period of 18 days, by which time the party was without food or water, the prisoners decided to kill the deceased, a cabin-boy, in order that they might eat his body. On the 20th day, Dudley, with the consent of Stephens killed the deceased, who because of his youth was in a weaker state than the other members of the party. The three survivors lived on the flesh of the deceased for a further four days after which they were picked up by a passing ship. At the time the boy was killed there was no prospect of rescue and it appeared that unless the prisoners ate the deceased they would die of starvation. Counsel argued the defence of necessity. Lord Coleridge C.J. stated:

"It must not be supposed that in refusing to admit temptation to be an excuse for crime, it is forgotten how terrible the temptation was: how awful the suffering; how hard in such trials to keep the judgement straight and the conduct pure. We are often compelled to set up standards we cannot reach ourselves and to lay down rules which we could not ourselves satisfy. But a man has no right to declare temptation to be an excuse, though he might himself have yielded to it, nor to allow compassion for the criminal to change or weaken in any manner the legal definition of the crime. It is therefore our duty to declare that the prisoners' act in this case was wilful murder, that the facts as stated in the verdict are no legal justification of the homicide; and to say that in our unanimous opinion the prisoners are upon this special verdict guilty of murder."

The accused were sentenced to death, but the sentence was later commuted to six months imprisonment.

75. R v Lipman (1969) – Lipman and a girl were drug addicts and one evening, after he had consumed a quantity of LSD in her room, he began to suffer hallucinations and he had an hallucination in which he descended to the centre of the earth and fought off attacking snakes. Whilst on his "trip" he struck the girl several severe blows and stuffed about eight inches of sheet in her mouth causing her to suffocate. Lipman was charged with murder and pleaded that he had no knowledge of what he was doing whilst under the influence of the drug and that he had no intention of harming the deceased. He was convicted of manslaughter and appealed. It was held that the conviction must stand. Lord Justice Widgery said:

"For the purposes of criminal responsibility we see no reason to distinguish between the effect of drugs voluntarily taken and drunkenness voluntarily induced. As to the latter there is a great deal of authority.

We can dispose of the present application by reiterating that when the killing results from an unlawful act of the prisoner no specific intent has to be proved to convict of manslaughter, and self-induced intoxication is accordingly no defence. Since in the present case the acts complained of were obviously likely to cause harm to the victim and did, in fact, kill her no acquittal was possible and the verdict of manslaughter was inevitable."

76. R v Lamb (1967) – Lamb was charged with manslaughter. He was inexperienced in the use of firearms and as a practical joke, with no intention to cause harm, he pointed a revolver at the deceased, his best friend, when it had two bullets in the chambers. Neither bullet was in the chamber opposite the barrel and Lamb did not know that the act of pulling the trigger would cause the cylinder to rotate with the result that one of the bullets would be brought under the firing pin. Three expert witnesses for the prosecution agreed that the mistake was natural for someone who was unaware of the manner in which a revolver worked. The trial judge refused to allow the defence of accident to go to the jury and the appellant was convicted of manslaughter. It was held that the conviction should be quashed on the ground that when the basis of a charge is criminal negligence or recklessness of the accused, the jury must consider his state of mind, including whether or not the thought that the act which he was doing was safe, and the trial judge had not directed the jury on this matter. The appellant was entitled to a direction that the jury should take into account the fact that he had indisputably formed the view that there was no danger, and that there was expert evidence as to that being an understandable mistake. Strong though the evidence of criminal negligence was, the appellant was entitled as of right to have his defence considered but he was not accorded this right and the jury was left without a direction on an essential matter. The appeal was therefore allowed.

77. R v Spurge (1961) – Spurge was driving his Ferrari sports car round a dangerous sharp left-hand bend at a reasonable speed when he was forced to apply the brakes rather sharply and the car swerved out of control, crossed the double white lines in the centre of the road and collided with a motor scooter approaching on the opposite side of the road. Spurge had purchased the car only a few days previously, but he had noticed that the brakes had a tendency to pull the car to the right. He was convicted of dangerous driving contrary to Section 11(1) of the Road Traffic Act 1930 and appealed, maintaining that he was not guilty of the offence since the cause of the accident was the defective brakes and not the manner in which he was driving. It was held by the Court of Criminal Appeal that the conviction would be affirmed on the ground that he knew that the car had a tendency to swerve to the right when the brakes were applied and the defence of mechanical defect could not succeed since it was dangerous to drive the car with full knowledge of the mechanical defect.

78. R v Turner (1971) – Turner took his car to Brown's garage to be repaired. When the work was done, Turner told Brown that he would return the next day to pay for the repairs and to take the car away. A few hours later, however, without telling Brown, he took the car from where it had been parked on the road outside the garage. The loss was reported to the police and the car was later discovered near Turner's home. Turner later admitted to the police that he had taken the car away without paying, but alleged that he had Brown's consent. At the trial the judge directed the jury:
(1) the sole question was whether Brown had possession or control of the car, and
(2) in order to find Turner guilty it was essential to prove he had acted dishonestly and it was immaterial that he had no basis in law for his belief that he had a claim or right to the car.

It was held that the jury had been properly directed and the appeal would be dismissed by the Court of Appeal. Lord Parker C.J. stated that "The words 'belonging to another' are specifically defined in Section 5 of the Theft Act 1968. Section 5(1) provides: property shall be regarded as belonging to any person having possession or control of it, or having in it any proprietary right or interest."

The judge directed the jury that they were not concerned in any way with lien and the sole question was whether the garage owner had possession or control. This court is quite satisfied that there is no ground whatever for qualifying the words "possession or control" in any way. It is sufficient if it is found that the person from whom the property is taken, or to use the words of the Act, appropriated, was at the time in fact in possession or control.

The second point related to the necessity for proving dishonesty. This court is, however, quite satisfied that there is nothing in this point whatever. The whole test of dishonesty is the mental element of belief. No doubt, although the appellant may for certain purposes be presumed to know the law, he would not at the time have the vaguest idea whether he did have in law a right to take the car back again, and accordingly when one looks at his mental state, one looks at it in the light of what he believed. The jury were properly told that if he believed that he had a right, albeit there was none, he would nevertheless fall to be acquitted.

79. R v Warner (1970) – Mr Thorne, a service engineer left his tool-box near the door of the workshop where he was employed. A short time later he saw Warner carrying a tool-box which looked like his property. Mr Thorne then saw that his tool-box had gone and Warner was charged with the theft of the tool-box and its contents. Warner said that he had taken the tool-box because of unpleasantness between him and others who had obstructed his right of way and he intended to take the box and return it after about an hour to get his own back. He was convicted and appealed. It was held that the conviction should be quashed as a result of a misdirection by the trial judge with regard to the meaning of "intention permanently to deprive". The Court stated that the Theft Act 1968 had not forsaken the basic conception of both the common law and earlier legislation that there can be no theft without the intention of permanently depriving another of his property and a jury should receive a clear direction on this ingredient of the offence of theft.

80. Director of Public Prosecutions v Withers (1974) – Withers and others operated an investigation agency. In order to make reports for clients about the status and financial standing of third parties, the appellants obtained confidential information from banks, building societies, government departments and local authorities. The information was obtained by telephone and to obtain information about bank accounts and criminal records a number of lies were told. The appellants were

CRIMINAL LAW

indicted on a charge of conspiracy to effect a public mischief and the jury were directed that an agreement to do deceitful acts which could cause extreme injury to the community as a whole amounted to the offence with which they were charged. They were convicted and appealed unsuccessfully to the Court of Appeal, but the Court certified that a point of law of general public importance was involved namely:

"Whether the learned judge was right in law in stating that if the jury were sure that one of the appellants agreed with another appellant to do wilfully deceitful acts themselves or agreed to procure others to do such wilfully deceitful acts for them, and that such wilfully deceitful acts would cause extreme injury to the general well-being of the community as a whole, such persons who so agreed would be guilty of the offence of conspiring to effect a public mischief."

In the House of Lords, Viscount Dilhorne summed up:

"To say that there is now no power in the judges to declare new offences does not, of course, mean that well-established principles are not to be applied to new facts. Fraud, like contempt of court, may take many forms and a conviction for conspiracy to defraud may well be sustained though the fraud has taken a novel form. ...

What conclusions are to be drawn from the cases to which I have referred? I think they are these: (1) There is no separate and distinct class of criminal conspiracy called conspiracy to effect a public mischief. (2) That description has in the past been applied to a number of cases which might have been regarded as coming within well-known heads of conspiracy, e.g. conspiracy to defraud, to pervert the course of justice etc. (3) It is far too late to hold that conspiracy of the kind that occurred in those cases was not criminal and Lord Goddard's observations in Newland should be understood in that sense. (4) The judges have no power to create new offences. (5) Where a charge of conspiracy to effect a public mischief has been preferred, the question to be considered is whether the object or means of conspiracy are in substance of such a kind or quality as has already been recognised by the law as criminal. (6) If they are, then one has to go on to consider, on an appeal, whether the trial took in consequence of the reference to public mischief was such as to vitiate the conviction.

Relating these conclusions to the appeal, it may be that, if the references to public mischief had been omitted from counts 1 and 2 of the indictment, the case might have proceeded on the basis that the conspiracy charged in each count was the conspiracy to defraud, and if the accused had then been convicted, then by applying the reasoning of Lord Radcliffe in Welham v D.P.P. and the dictum of Lord Tucker in Board of Trade v Owen the convictions could have been upheld. In my opinion it cannot be said in this case as it was in Bailey that the reference to public mischief did not vitiate the trial.

I hope that in future such a vague expression as 'public mischief' will not be included in criminal charges. It introduces a wide measure of uncertainty and should not be a vehicle for the enlargement of the criminal law or a device to secure its extension to cover acts not previously thought to be criminal.

In my opinion, this appeal should be allowed."

81. R v Franklin (1883) – Franklin took a box from Brighton pier and threw it over into the sea. Several people were swimming around the pier at that time and one boy was struck on the head by the box and killed. The prosecution maintained that if death followed consequently upon a tortious act, then it is manslaughter. The judge directed the jury that the civil wrong committed against the refreshment stall keeper was immaterial in establishing criminal liability. Franklin was convicted of manslaughter.

82. R v Blaue (1975) – An 18-year-old girl was a Jehovah's witness and strictly obeyed the doctrines of that sect. One evening the appellant visited her and requested sexual intercourse. Being of religious disposition, she refused and the appellant attacked her with a knife, causing a serious stab wound which pierced her lung. She declined a blood transfusion because it was contrary to her religious beliefs, in spite of being told that she would die if she persisted in her refusal, and died the following day. The appellant was acquitted of murder but convicted of manslaughter on the ground of diminished responsibility. He was also convicted of wounding with intent to cause grievous bodily harm and indecent assault. He appealed against the conviction for manslaughter, contending that the refusal to have a blood transfusion was unreasonable and broke the chain of causation between the stabbing and the death. Lawton L.J. in the Court of Appeal, Criminal Division stated:

"When the judge came to direct the jury on this issue, he did so by telling them that they should apply their common sense. He then went on to tell them they would get some help from the cases to which counsel had referred in their speeches. He reminded them of what Lord Parker C.J. had said in R v Smith and what Maule J. had said 133 years before in R v Holland. He placed particular reliance on what the latter judge had said. The jury he said, might find it 'most material and helpful'." He went on, "This is one of those relatively rare cases, you may think, with very little option open to you but to reach the conclusion that was reached by your predecessors as members of the jury in R v Holland, namely 'Yes' to the question of causation that the stab was still, at the time of the girl's death, the operating cause of death, or a substantial cause of death. However, that is a matter for you to determine after you have withdrawn to consider your verdicts.' Counsel, for the appellant had criticised this direction on three grounds: first, because R v Holland should no longer be considered good law; secondly, because R v Smith, when rightly understood, does envisage the possibility of unreasonable conduct on the part of the victim breaking the chain of causation; and thirdly, because the judge in reality directed the jury to find causation proved although he used words which seemed to leave the issue open for them to decide.

In R v Holland, the defendant, in the course of a violent assault, had injured one of his victim's fingers. A surgeon had advised amputation because of danger to life through complications developing. The advice was rejected. A fortnight later the victim died of lockjaw. ... The real question is, said Maule J. 'whether in the end the wound inflicted by the prisoner was the cause of death?' That distinguished judge left the jury to decide the question, by pooling their experience of life and using their common sense.

Maule J.'s direction to the jury reflected the common law's answer to the problem. He who inflicted an injury which resulted in death could not excuse himself by pleading that his victim could have avoided death by taking greater care of himself.

There have been two cases in recent years which have some bearing on this topic: R v Jordan and R v Smith. In R v Jordan, the Court of Criminal Appeal, after conviction, admitted some medical evidence which went on to prove that the cause of death was not the blow relied on by the prosecution but abnormal medical treatment after admission to hospital. This case has been criticised but it was probably rightly decided on its facts. Before the abnormal treatment started the injury had almost healed. We share Lord Parker C.J.'s opinion that R v Jordan should be regarded as a case decided on its own special facts and not as an authority relaxing the common law approach to causation. Lord Parker C.J. in the course of his judgement, commented as follows: 'It seems to the Court that if, at the time of death, the original wound is still an operating cause and a substantial cause, then the death can properly be said to be a result of the wound, albeit that some other cause of death is operating. Only if it can be said that the original wounding is merely the setting in which another cause operates can it be said that the death does not result from the wound. Putting it another way, only if the second cause is so overwhelming as to make the original wound merely part of the history can it be said that death does not flow from the wound.'

The physical cause of death in this case was the bleeding into the pleural cavity arising from the penetration of the lung. This had not been brought about by any decision made by the deceased girl but by the stab wound.

Counsel for the appellant tried to overcome this line of reasoning by submitting that the jury should have been directed that if they thought the girl's decision not to have a blood transfusion was an unreasonable one then the chain of causation would have been broken. At once the question arises − reasonable by whose standards? Those of Jehovah's witnesses? Humanists? Roman Catholics? Protestants of Anglo-Saxon descent? The man on the Clapham omnibus?

As was pointed out to counsel for the appellant in the course of argument, two cases, each raising the same issue of reasonableness, because of religious beliefs, could produce different verdicts, depending on where the cases were tried. A jury drawn from Preston, sometimes said to be the most Catholic town in England, might have different views about martyrdom to one drawn from the inner suburbs of London. Counsel for the appellant accepted that this might be so: it was, he said, inherent in trial by jury. It is not inherent in the common law as expounded by Sir Matthew Hale and Maule J. It has long been the policy of the law that those who use violence on other people must take their victims as they find them. This in our judgement means the whole man, not just the physical man. It does not lie in the mouth of the assailant to say that his victim's religious beliefs which inhibited him from accepting certain kinds of treatment were unreasonable. The question for decision is what caused her death. The answer is the stab wound. The fact that the victim refused to stop this end coming about did not break the causal connection between the act and death." Accordingly the appeal was dismissed.

83. R v Evans (1962) − Evans, an experienced driver with a long and good record was driving his Jaguar along a straight open road and decided to overtake another motor car travelling ahead of him at about 40 miles an hour. Evans increased his speed to about 60 miles per hour, went on the wrong side of the road and crashed head-on into a motor car approaching from the opposite direction. The driver of the other car was killed. Evans did not see the approaching car as there was a dip in the road and the car was hidden by the dip when he started to overtake. However, he knew that the dip was there and he decided to take a chance. He was convicted of causing death by dangerous driving and appealed to the Court of Criminal Appeal. It was held that his conviction would be affirmed as if a person adopts a manner of driving which the jury thinks is dangerous to other users of the road in all the circumstances, it matters not whether he was deliberately reckless, careless, momentarily inattentive or even doing his incompetent best.

84. R v Gosney (1971) – Mrs Gosney was stopped by the police when driving in the wrong direction down a dual carriageway. She had turned right into a road with which she was unfamiliar and was charged with dangerous driving contrary to Section 2(1) of the Road Traffic Act 1960. She attempted to prove at her trial by the production of plans and photographs that it was through no fault of her own that she was driving on the wrong carriageway, that there was nothing which would have indicated to a competent and careful driver in the circumstances prevailing that she was about to drive her car on the wrong side of the road. The trial judge would not allow her to adduce evidence in support of her contention because he took the view that driving in a manner dangerous to the public was an absolute offence. Mrs Gosney was convicted, but she successfully appealed to the Court of Appeal. Megaw L.J. stated:

"The deputy chairman agrees to have accepted that a driver would be guilty of dangerous driving even if the fact were that he had been positively directed by a road sign which had been turned the wrong way round, to travel in the wrong direction. It would mean that a driver would be guilty of dangerous driving, where, as a result of an obstruction in the highway, he had been affirmatively directed by a police officer to travel on the wrong carriageway and there, without any lack of care on his part, collided with a car travelling in the opposite direction, the police having omitted to stop or warn traffic coming from that direction.

It may well be thought that, if that is indeed the law, while it may lead towards certainty, it offends the sense of justice. The deputy chairman dealt with that aspect by saying 'The practical answer is that there would be no prosecution'. That is not much comfort to the accused if a prosecution is brought and he is precluded from proving the facts by cross-examination or direct evidence. By way of background, it may also be said that in an enactment designed primarily to promote safe and careful driving it is unlikely that Parliament intended to subject to the risk of convicting a driver who is doing nothing contrary to the standard of a competent and careful driver.

As has been said, the deputy chairman's ruling excluding the evidence was founded on what was said in R v Ball, R v Loughlin. In that case these words were used:

'It has been held time and again that an offence under this section is an absolute offence ... it is a liability on the driver which he cannot get rid of, and if the result of his driving produced what the jury consider to be a dangerous situation, a dangerous manoeuvre, then even though he had been completely blameless, he can be held liable.'

A little later was said:

'The case of Evans now sets out quite clearly that the test is a purely objective one and it matters not why the dangerous situation was caused or the dangerous manoeuvre executed.'

With very great respect, we disagree with both those passages. We do not think that they represent correctly the law as it has been stated in the authorities. We do not accept that the offence of dangerous driving is 'an absolute offence'. We do not accept that a driver who has been completely blameless can be held guilty. We do not accept that 'it matters not why the dangerous situation was caused'.

We would state briefly what in our judgement the law was and is on this question of fault in the offence of driving in a dangerous manner. It is not an absolute offence. In order to justify a conviction there must be, not only a situation which, viewed objectively was dangerous, but there must also have been some fault on the part of the driver, causing that situation. 'Fault' certainly does not necessarily involve deliberate misconduct or recklessness or intention to drive in a manner inconsistent with proper standards of driving. Nor does fault necessarily involve moral blame. Thus, there is fault if an inexperienced or a naturally poor driver, while straining every nerve to do the right thing, falls below the standard of a competent and careful driver. Fault involves a failure; a falling below the care or skill of a competent and experienced driver, in relation to the manner of the driving and the relevant circumstances of the case. A fault in that sense, even though it might be slight, even though it be a momentary lapse, even though, normally no danger would have arisen from it, is sufficient." The appeal was allowed.

85. Director of Public Prosecutions v Ray (1973) – Ray, a university student, and three friends went to a Chinese restaurant in Gainsborough and ordered a meal valued at 47 pence. When the order was given, Ray intended to pay for the meal. The meal was served and eaten, and there were no complaints about the quality or quantity of food. The four friends had a discussion and decided not to pay, they therefore waited until the waiter had left the room and during his absence in the kitchen they ran out of the restaurant without paying. Ray was convicted of dishonestly obtaining a pecuniary advantage by deception contrary to the Theft Act 1968 Section 16(1). The conviction was quashed by the Divisional Court of the Queen's Bench Division and the Crown appealed. Per Lord Morris of Borth-y-Gest:

"In the present case it is found as a fact that when the respondent ordered his meal he believed that he would be able to pay. One of his companions had agreed to lend him money. He therefore intended to pay. So far as the waiter was concerned the original implied representation made to him by the respondent must have been a continuing representation so long as he remained in the restaurant. There was nothing to alter the representation. Just as the waiter was led at the start to believe that he was dealing with a customer who by all that he did in the restaurant was indicating his intention to pay in the ordinary way, so the waiter was led to believe that the state of affairs continued. But the moment came when the respondent decided and therefore knew that he was not going to pay; but he also knew that the waiter still thought he was going to pay. By ordering his meal and by his conduct on assuming the role of an ordinary customer the respondent had previously shown that it was his intention to pay. By continuing in the same role and behaving just as before he was representing that his previous intention continued. That was a deception because his intention, unknown to the waiter, had become quite otherwise. The dishonest change of intention was not likely to produce the result that the waiter would be told of it. The essence of the deception was that the waiter should not know of it or be given any sort of clue that it (the change of intention) had come about. Had the waiter suspected that by a change of intention a secret exodus was being planned, it is obvious that he would have taken action to prevent it being achieved.

It was said in the Divisional Court that a deception under section 16 should not be found unless an accused has actively made a representation by words or conduct which representation is found to be false. But if there was an original representation (as, in my view, there was when the meal was ordered) it was a representation that was intended to be and was a continuing representation. It continued to operate on the mind of the waiter. It became false and it became a deliberate deception. The prosecution do not say that the deception consisted in not informing the waiter of the change in mind: they say that the deception consisted in continuing to represent to the waiter that there was an intention to pay before leaving.

On behalf of the respondent it was contended that no deception was practised. It was accepted that when the meal was ordered there was a representation by the respondent that he would pay, but it was contended that once the meal was served there was no longer any representation that there was merely an obligation to pay a debt: it was further argued that thereafter there was no deception because there was no obligation in the debtor to inform his creditor that payment was not to be made. I cannot accept these contentions. They ignore the circumstances that the representation that was made was a continuing one: its essence was that the intention to pay would continue until payment was made: by its very nature it could not cease to operate as a representation unless some new arrangement was made.

A further contention on behalf of the respondent was that the debt was not in the whole or in part evaded. It was said that on the facts found there was an evasion of the payment of a debt and that a debt (which denotes an obligation to pay) is not evaded unless it is released or unless there is a discharge of it which is void or voidable. I cannot accept this contention. Though a 'debt' as referred to in the section does denote an obligation to pay, the obligation of the respondent was to pay for his meal before he left the restaurant. When he left without paying he had, in my view, evaded his obligation to pay before leaving. He dodged his obligation. Accordingly he obtained a 'pecuniary advantage'.

The final question which arises is whether, if there was deception and there was pecuniary advantage, it was by the deception that the respondent obtained the pecuniary advantage. In my view, this must be a question of fact and the magistrates have found that it was by his deception that the respondent dishonestly evaded payment. It would seem to be clear that if the waiter had thought that if he left the restaurant to go to the kitchen the respondent would at once run out, he (the waiter) would not have left the restaurant and would have taken suitable action. The waiter proceeded on the basis that the implied representation made to him (i.e. of an honest intention to pay) was effective. The waiter was caused to refrain from taking certain courses of action which but for the representation he would have taken. In my view, the respondent during the whole time that he was in the restaurant made and by his continuing conduct continued to make a representation of his intention to pay before leaving. When in place of his original intention he substituted the dishonest intention of running away as soon as the waiter's back was turned, he was continuing to lead the waiter to believe that he intended to pay. He practised a deception on the waiter and by doing so he obtained for himself the pecuniary advantage of evading his obligation to pay before leaving. That he did so dishonestly was found by the magistrates, who, in my opinion, rightly convicted him. I would allow the appeal."

86. Fairclough v Whipp (1951) – The respondent was charged with having unlawfully and indecently assaulted a girl under 16 years of age, contrary to the Offences against the Person Act 1861 Section 52. He had invited a child of nine years of age to touch his person, and she had done so. He was acquitted. Lord Goddard stated:

"An assault can be constituted, without there being battery, for instance, by a threatening gesture or a threat to use violence against a person, but I do not know any authority which says that where one person invites another person to touch him that can be said to be an assault. The question of consent or non-consent only arises if there is something which can be called an assault and without consent would be an assault. If that which was done to the child was of an indecent nature and would have been an assault if done against her will, it would also be an assault if it was done with her consent because she could not consent to an indecent assault. Before we decide whether there has been an indecent assault we must decide whether there has been an assault and I cannot hold that an invitation to somebody to touch the invitor can amount to an assault on the invitee."

N.B. Such conduct would now amount to a crime under the Indecency with Children Act 1960.

PRACTICE QUESTIONS

1. (a) Explain the terms "actus reus" and "mens rea".
   (b) Wilf puts four gallons of petrol into his car at a self-service petrol station. He is about to drive off without paying when an attendant attempts to stop him. Wilf shouts out, "I will pay you next week" and drives off. He is arrested next morning. Advise Wilf as to his criminal liability. (AEB 1979)
2. Jill wakes one night to find a burglar in her room. She throws a heavy silver candlestick at him which fractures his skull. If he dies, will she be guilty of either murder or manslaughter, or neither? Discuss. (AEB Nov 1972)
3. After snatching Joan's handbag, James collided with Peter who struck his head on a nearby lamp standard. Two days later Peter died in hospital. State with reasons what offences, if any, James could be charged with. (AEB Jun 1977)
4. Outline the main differences between a crime and a civil wrong.
5. Bill, aged 14, takes a bottle of brandy from a boat moored at the marina. Mr Smith, the owner of the boat, sees Bill taking it. What offence, if any, has Bill committed? Can Mr Smith arrest him?
6. (a) What does society hope to achieve by punishing its criminal offenders?
   (b) How far are these hopes achieved by the following:
       (1) The death penalty
       (2) Borstal training
       (3) A Community Service Order
       (4) An order depriving a person of property used in the commission of a crime? (AEB "A" Level)
7. (a) What is meant by "theft"?
   (b) Fred, a taxi-driver, agrees to take Mario, an Italian student, to

his destination, telling him that it is a rather complicated and difficult journey. In reality Mario's destination is less than two miles away and Fred demands £7 payment for the 50 pence journey. What offences, if any, can Fred be charged with? (AEB "O" Level)

8. Define "murder". What is meant by "malice aforethought" and "under the Queen's Peace"?
9. What is meant by the term "absolute offence". What justification exists for imposing absolute liability on certain offences?
10. Sylvia invites her friend Jim to visit her in her room at boarding school one night. Access to the room was to be via a balcony which ran the length of the building and in order to assist Jim's entry she promised to leave her window ajar. Jim accepts the invitation. On the appointed night Jim gained access to the balcony and seeing an open window clambers through it and enters what he thinks is Sylvia's room. The occupant of the room, Irene, thinking that it is her boyfriend, submits to his advances, but after a short time realises it is someone else and asks him to desist. Jim still thinking it is his girlfriend has sexual intercourse with her, only realising later that he has entered the wrong room. Jim is now charged with burglary and rape. Advise him.
11. What is the procedure involved in a case brought before the magistrates' court?
12. Explain what is meant by the maxim "Actus non facit reum nisi mens sit rea"? Say why this maxim is important in criminal law. What is the mens rea in murder?
13. Discuss Summons and Warrant. What considerations should influence a justice in deciding whether to issue a summons or a warrant in the first instance?
14. Distinguish between (i) An affray (ii) An unlawful assembly (iii) A rout (iv) A riot.
15. Fred is ordered by a well-known member of the I.R.A. who is reputably a ruthless gunman to drive him and two others in a hi-jacked car. Fred believes he will be shot if he disobeys and accordingly drives the men. He is suddenly told to stop and the three men get out of the car, shoot and fatally wound an off-duty policeman who is working on his car. The men return to Fred's car and order him to drive them away, which he does. Discuss.

WORKED EXAMPLES

4. Outline the main differences between a crime and a civil wrong.

The essential feature of a crime is that it is an offence against the community or state, whilst a civil wrong concerns only the individuals involved in the offence. The reason for certain offences being classified as crimes is that if they were allowed to proliferate unchecked they would lead to the ultimate collapse of public order. Naturally some offences such as assault are classified as crimes, but also allow the injured person a civil action in tort to recover compensation for his injuries.

As a crime is an offence against the state, criminal proceedings are commenced in the Queen's name, usually referred to as Regina versus Smith written R v Smith. In civil cases the party injured, the plaintiff, must commence action against the party causing the injury, the defendant, e.g., Smith v James.

Except for police discretion in minor criminal cases criminal proceedings are mandatory and once set in motion cannot be withdrawn. Court action in a civil matter is at the option of the party injured and proceedings may be ended or allowed to lapse at any time.

The object of prosecuting a criminal is to ensure that he is punished for his offence and if possible reformed, whilst his sentence acts as a deterrent to other members of society. Civil proceedings are taken solely with the purpose of compensating the plaintiff for the injury suffered.

The venue of trial also differs. All criminal proceedings commence in a magistrates' court, minor cases are tried, more serious cases are committed to the Crown Court. The less important civil cases are commenced in the County Court, the more important in the High Court.

Finally, except as provided by statute, there is no time limit in which criminal proceedings may be commenced, whereas civil actions are subject to strict limits.

5. Bill, aged 14, takes a bottle of brandy from a boat moored at the marina. Mr Smith, the owner of the boat sees Bill taking it. What offence, if any, has Bill committed? Can Mr Smith arrest him?

By the Children and Young Persons Act 1963 Section 16(1) there is an irrebuttable presumption that persons under the age of ten are incapable of crime. Children between the ages of ten and 14 are presumed incapable of criminal intent, but this presumption can be rebutted if the court is satisfied that the child knew what he was doing and he knew that this was wrong. Persons over 14 years of age, but under 18 have full criminal responsibility although there are certain differences in the method of trial, punishment and treatment from the adult offender.

Bill therefore has full criminal liability and the points to be considered are (1) Has he the requisite mens rea? and (2) Has he committed the appropriate actus reus? Section 1 of the Theft Act 1968 lays down that a person is guilty of theft if he dishonestly appropriates property belonging to another with the intention of permanently depriving that other of it. By Section 2 of the Act a person is not guilty of theft if he appropriates property (i) In the belief that he has a right to it (ii) Believing that he would have the owner's consent to take if the owner knew or (iii) If he believed that the owner could not be found by taking reasonable steps. By Section 3 of the Act, any assumption of the rights of an owner amounts to theft.

As Bill has actually taken the brandy, he has performed the actus reus (criminal act) and there will be strong evidence that he intends to permanently deprive Mr Smith of the brandy. If Mr Smith stopped him in the Act then Bill would at least be guilty of an attempt to steal. The facts do not indicate that any of the defences in Section 2 are available and the offences are therefore theft or attempted theft.

Theft is punishable by imprisonment for more than five years and is therefore an arrestable offence under the provisions of the Criminal Law Act 1967. The Theft Act specifically states that theft is an arrestable offence so the academic point that as a person under 17 cannot be normally given a prison sentence he perhaps is not guilty of an arrestable offence is therefore avoided.

The case of Christie v Leachinsky (1947) decided that "any person may arrest without warrant anyone who is, or whom he, with reasonable cause, suspects to be in the act of committing an arrestable offence". As Mr Smith saw Bill commit the offence, he clearly has power to arrest and as the grounds of arrest are obvious he has no need to give Bill any reasons for his action.

11. What is the procedure involved in a case brought before a magistrates' court?

A criminal case may be commenced by the laying of information that a person has or is suspected of having committed an offence against the criminal law. The magistrate may either issue a summons directed to the person requiring him to appear before the Magistrates' Court on the date stated to answer to the information or a warrant, which is a direction for the arrest of that person so that he can be brought before the Court. A warrant should not of course be issued where a summons would be equally effective except in cases of a grave nature and there are special rules as to when a magistrate must not issue a warrant. The information need not be on oath or in writing unless a warrant is requested.

When the accused appears, he will have the substance of the information read out to him and be asked whether he pleads guilty or not guilty and in cases where he has an option if he wishes to be tried summarily.

If the magistrates are sitting as examining magistrates they will decide whether or not to commit him to Crown Court for trial. The prosecution will in either event offer their evidence but if it is just committal procedure, the person accused may decide to retain his evidence for production in the Crown Court. In due course the accused will be entitled to have a copy of the record of evidence called "depositions" and also of the information itself so that his solicitor may study these in the Crown Court. The process ends when the Court either dismisses the information, commits for trial or tries the case and convicts and sentences the accused. If the accused is committed for trial a formal indictment is then prepared which commences the proceedings in the Crown Court.

2. Jill wakes one night to find a burglar in her room. She throws a heavy silver candlestick at him which fractures his skull. If he dies will she be guilty of either murder or manslaughter, or neither? Discuss.

If Jill is charged with murder the prosecution must prove beyond all reasonable doubt (Woolmington v D.P.P. 1935) that she has committed the unlawful killing of a reasonable creature (a human) in being (born alive) and under the Queen's Peace (not in an act of war) with malice aforethought (intent to do the act) express or implied the death following within a year and a day (the injured burglar must die within this period).

Manslaughter is the unlawful killing of another without malice aforethought and is of two kinds – voluntary such as when a person kills in the heat of the moment under provocation and involuntary manslaughter where death results from an act by a person who did not intend to kill or cause grievous bodily harm but nevertheless intended some lesser degree of harm. Manslaughter may also be committed where a person does an act which is in itself quite lawful with such gross negligence as to amount to recklessness. The negligence must show such disregard for life and safety of others as to amount to a crime against the state and conduct deserving punishment.

We are however told that the intruder is a burglar and from the definition of this offence, we know that he is on the premises as a trespasser with intent to commit an offence of theft, inflict grievous bodily harm, rape or inflict unlawful damage or that having entered the building as a trespasser has stolen or attempted to steal or inflicted or attempted to inflict grievous bodily harm on any person therein.

Both in the case of murder and manslaughter, self-defence may be a defence of justification, i.e., make the killing lawful. A person is entitled to use reasonable force in defence of himself or others, or in defence of his property. From the above definition of burglary either the person or property of Jill is threatened and as she is in bed she cannot retreat and will be justified in using whatever means are available to repel her attacker. Although she can be charged with murder or manslaughter she is not guilty of either.

3. After snatching Joan's handbag, James collided with Peter who struck his head on a nearby lamp standard. Two days later Peter died in hospital. State with reason, what offences, if any, James could be charged with.

In order for a person to be convicted of a criminal offence the prosecution must prove two things beyond all reasonable doubt, namely the mens rea, or intent to commit the act and the actus reus, or criminal act.

CRIMINAL LAW

If we apply these requirements to the facts of the question it is fairly obvious that in snatching the handbag, James intended to deprive Joan permanently of her handbag as is required by Section 1 of the Theft Act 1968. There was a dishonest appropriation with no claim of right in good faith. As the violence applied was merely in furtherance of the taking of the handbag and not with the object of putting Joan in fear, the act is one of simple theft and not robbery.

Regarding the collision with Peter, this was unintentional although negligent and as everyman is presumed to intend the natural consequences of his act (and the question does say with what offences can he be charged) it is possible that he could be charged with murder although the absence of mens rea means that the prosecution would be unlikely to succeed. It is more likely that a charge of manslaughter will succeed. Manslaughter is the unlawful killing of another without malice aforethought. Involuntary manslaughter is where death results from an act by the accused which was not intended to kill or cause grievous bodily harm but nevertheless intended some degree of harm. Manslaughter may be committed where a person does an act which in itself is quite lawful, but does that act with such gross negligence as to amount to reckless. The negligence must show such disregard for the life and safety of others as to amount to a crime against the State and conduct deserving of punishment.

James may of course be charged with and convicted of the lesser offences of assault and battery or if any malice was present, the offence of malicious wounding.

12. Explain what is meant by the maxim "Actus non facit reum nisi mens sit rea". Say why this maxim is important in criminal law. What is the mens rea in murder?

The maxim "Actus non facit reum, nisi mens sit rea" means the act itself does not constitute guilt unless done with a guilty intent. Thus the words refer to the mental element necessary in a crime. The maxim is very important in criminal law because it refers to the fact that the performance of a guilty act is not alone the requisite necessary for a crime. The "mens rea" – the guilty mind or mental element – in crimes is most important, although there are certain statutory exceptions in particular relating to motoring offences (Harding v Price 1948; Strowger v John 1975). Thus, if A sees a book on a table and believing this to be his own (but in fact, it belongs to B) takes it home with him, he has done the guilty act, but has not the necessary mental element (the "mens rea") for it to be a crime. If he finds out later that it is not his book and then decides to keep it, the situation is different; he then has the necessary "mens rea" and, according to the circumstances could be convicted of theft.

The statutory definition of murder is the "unlawful killing of a reasonable creature who is in being and under the Queen's peace, with malice aforethought ... death following within a year and a day". The particular mens rea necessary is embodied in the phrase "with malice aforethought". This is peculiar to murder and distinguishes it from other homicides (for example manslaughter). In any trial where murder is the charge the malice aforethought (that is the actual intention to murder) has to be proved. The test of intent is now subjective (C.J.A. 1967 Section 8).

"A court or jury in determining whether a person has committed an offence: (a) Shall not be bound in law to infer that he intended or foresaw a result of his action by reason only of it being a natural or probable sequence of that action; but (b) Shall decide whether he did intend or foresee that result by reference to all the evidence, drawing such inferences from the evidence as appear proper in the circumstances."

14. Distinguish between (i) An affray (ii) An unlawful assembly (iii) A rout (iv) A riot.

An affray is committed by one or more persons fighting to the terror of the Queen's subjects. The offence need not necessarily take place in a public place (Button and Swain v D.P.P. 1966) but there must be bystanders who are put in fear. If no one is put in fear the police may arrest and prefer a lesser charge of assault or breach of the peace.

An unlawful assembly is a common law offence punishable by fine and imprisonment. It is committed when three or more people meet with a common purpose to commit a crime of violence or achieve some other object, whether legal or not in such a way as to cause reasonable men to apprehend a breach of the peace. A lawful assembly is not rendered unlawful merely because those taking part are aware that others opposed to it will probably cause a breach of the peace (Beatty v Gilbanks 1882). The case of Thomas v Sawkins (1955) established that a public meeting may be held on private premises.

Rout is another common law offence punishable by a fine and

imprisonment. It is committed when the members of the unlawful assembly proceed together towards their unlawful objective.

Once the unlawful assembly commences to carry out its illegal purpose intending to help one another by force if necessary, against anyone who may oppose them, or actually uses force or violence in such a way as to alarm at least one person of reasonable firmness and courage the common law offence of riot is committed.

15. Fred is ordered by a well-known member of the I.R.A. who is reputably a ruthless gunman to drive him and two others in a hi-jacked car. Fred believes he will be shot if he disobeys and accordingly drives the men. He is suddenly told to stop and the three men get out of the car shoot and fatally wound an off-duty policeman who is working on his car. The men return to Fred's car and order him to drive them away, which he does. Discuss.

The facts of the question closely resemble those of the case of Lynch v Director of Public Prosecutions for Northern Ireland (1975), in which Lynch was charged with murder, the case being that he was a principal in the second degree. He was convicted and appealed unsuccessfully to the Court of Appeal of Northern Ireland who held that duress could not be a defence to a charge of murder. The Court gave Lynch leave to appeal to the House of Lords, certifying that two points of law of general public importance were involved in their decision. The first question certified was whether on a charge of murder the defence of duress is open to a person "who is accused as a principal in the second degree (aider and abettor)". The House gave an affirmative answer to this; see Abbot v R (1976). The second question was:

"Where a person charged with murder as an aider and abettor is shown to have intentionally done an act which assists in the commission of the murder with knowledge that the probable result of his act, combined with the acts of those whom his act is assisting, will be the death or serious bodily injury of another, is his guilt thereby established without the necessity of proving his willingness to participate in the crime?"

In answering this question Lord Morris of Borth-y-Gest said:

"If in the present case the jury were satisfied that the car was driven towards the garage in pursuance of a murderous plan and that the appellant knew that that was the plan and intentionally drove the car in execution of that plan he could be held to have aided and abetted even though he regretted the plan or indeed was horrified by it. However great his reluctance he would have intended to aid and abet. But if that intention and all that he did only came about because of the compulsion of duress of the nature that I have described he would, in my view, have a defence."

It was held by a majority that the appeal would be allowed and a new trial ordered as the trial judge's ruling was wrong. The two dissenting Law Lords stated that the drawing of an arbitrary line between murder as a principal in the first degree and murder as a principal in the second degree cannot be justified either morally or juridically.

13. Discuss Summons and Warrant. What considerations should influence a justice in deciding whether to issue a summons or a warrant in the first instance?

A summons and a warrant for arrest are both merely methods of securing the appearance of an alleged offender before the court. It is the duty of a justice to issue either a summons or a warrant whenever a charge or complaint is laid before him that a person has committed, or is suspected of having committed a criminal offence within his jurisdiction.

The issue of either a summons or warrant is discretionary on the part of the justice, and if his discretion is properly exercised the decision cannot be overruled by a higher court. Usually a warrant would not be issued in the first instance unless the alleged crime was serious or there was reasonable ground for suspecting that the accused would fail to answer a summons. If a summons is disobeyed, however, a warrant might well be issued.

If a justice is required to issue a warrant in the first instance, it is necessary that an information and complaint in writing should be laid before him on oath: whereas if a summons only is required to be issued, the information need not be in writing nor on oath.

Both a summons and a warrant are similar in form in that they both briefly state the offence charged although the summons is directed to the accused ordering him to appear at a certain time and place; whereas a warrant is directed to a constable ordering him to bring the accused to court.

10. Sylvia invites her boy-friend Jim to visit her in her room at boarding-school one night. Access to the room was to be via a balcony

which ran the length of the building and in order to assist Jim's entry, she promised to leave her window ajar. Jim accepts the invitation. On the appointed night, Jim gained access to the balcony and seeing an open window clambers through it and enters what he thinks is Sylvia's room. The occupant of the room, Irene, thinking that it is her boy-friend submits to his advances but after a short time realises it is someone else and asks him to desist. Jim still thinking that it is his girlfriend has sexual intercourse with her only realising later that he has entered the wrong room. Jim is now charged with burglary and rape. Advise him.

Section 9 of the Theft Act 1968 renders a person guilty of burglary if he enters any building or part of a building as a trespasser with intent to commit rape. The entry of the accused must therefore be proved and there is little doubt that Jim entered Irene's bedroom. Secondly, it must be proved that he entered as a trespasser and thirdly it must be proved that he entered as a trespasser with intent at the time of entry to commit rape therein.

Entry as a trespasser is a question which has not been settled in the courts, but in the case of R v Collins (1972) in which the facts had a similarity to those of the question, reference was made to Archbold's "Criminal Pleading, Evidence and Practice" which stated "Any intentional, negligent or reckless entry into a building will, it would appear, constitute a trespass if the building is in the possession of another person who does not consent to the entry. Nor will it make any difference if the entry was a result of a reasonable mistake, on the part of the defendant, so far as trespass is concerned." Edmund Davies L.J. disagreed with this interpretation and held that for the purpose of Section 9 of the Theft Act 1968 a person entering a building is not guilty of trespass if he enters without knowledge that he is trespassing or at least without acting recklessly as to whether or not he is unlawfully entering.

The jury would have to consider therefore whether or not Jim entered the room as a trespasser and in view of the previous instructions given by Sylvia it would appear that Jim has a good defence to the charge of burglary.

With regard to the charge of rape, reference must be made to the Sexual Offences (Amendment) Act 1976 which states that a man commits rape if:
(a) he has unlawful sexual intercourse with a woman who at the time of the intercourse does not consent to it; and

(b) at that time he knows that she does not consent to the intercourse or is reckless as to whether she consents to it.

The act continues to state that it is declared that if at a trial for a rape offence the jury has to consider whether a man believed that a woman was consenting to sexual intercourse, the presence or absence of reasonable grounds for such a belief is a matter to which the jury is to have regard in conjunction with any other relevant matters, in considering whether he so believed.

In view of this fact and in view of the decision in R v Collins it would appear that as Jim had reasonable grounds for believing that Irene consented to sexual intercourse he would have a good defence to a charge of rape.

GLOSSARY OF TERMS

Ab initio	– From the beginning
Actus non facit reum nisi mens sit rea	– An act itself does not make a man guilty unless he does it with a guilty intention
Actus reus	– A guilty act
A fortiori	– For a stronger reason
Alibi	– Elsewhere
Aliter	– Otherwise
Aliunde	– From elsewhere
A priori	– From effect to cause
Asportatio	– The act of carrying away
Autrefois Aquit	– The accused has been acquitted on another occasion in respect of that crime
Autrefois Convict	– The accused has been convicted of that crime on another occasion
Bona Fide	– In good faith
Consensus ad idem	– A mutual agreement by the parties
Contra bonos mores	– Contrary to good morals
Contraband	– A forbidden object
De facto	– In fact
De jure	– By right
De minimis non curat lex	– The Law does not concern itself with trifles
Deodand	– Instrument of crime – until 1846 this was forfeit to the Crown
Dictum	– Saying
Doli incapax	– Incapable of crime
Ex gratia	– Out of kindness
Felo de se	– Killed by one's own hand (suicide)
Flagrante Delicto	– In the fact of committing the offence

CRIMINAL LAW

Habeas corpus	– A writ addressed to one who is committing unlawful imprisonment commanding him to let the bearer have the body, i.e., release him
Ignorantia juris haud (non) excusat	– Ignorance of the law is no excuse
In delicto	– At fault
In loco parentis	– In the place of a parent
In minore delicto	– A person who is less at fault
Lex fori	– The law of the court in which the case is heard
Locus in quo	– The scene of the event
Mens rea	– A guilty intent
Nemo dat quod non habet	– No one can give a better title than he himself possesses
Non sequitur	– An inconsistent statement
Obiter Dictum	– Things said by the way, comments by judges which do not form part of the reasoning
Par delictum	– Equal fault
Pendente lite	– While a law suit is pending
Per curiam	– In the opinion of the court
Per incuriam	– Through oversight
Per se	– By itself
Post Mortem	– After death
Prima facie	– At first sight
Puisne	– Inferior
Ratio Decidendi	– The reason for the decision
Res judicata	– A matter on which the court has previously reached a decision
Sine die	– Without a day appointed – indefinitely
Turpis causa	– Immoral conduct
Vi et armis	– By force of arms

EXAMINATION TECHNIQUE

The approach to examinations is a personal thing. Some candidates like to revise till the last minute whilst others prefer to rest before the vital day.

Before entering the examination room, however, students should ensure that they keep up to date with current developments in the law by reading periodicals such as *The Law Quarterly Review*, *Law Notes*, copies of Law Reports relevant to the particular area of study and the law reports published in *The Times*. It is also useful to pay attention to radio and television programmes which give current opinion on various law topics.

In the examination room there are some points to remember which seem obvious but are frequently ignored and are often the cause of failure.

1. Ensure that you know the date, time and place of the examination.
2. Study previous papers of your particular examination so that you know how much time can be allowed to each question.
3. Read the rubrics (instructions) carefully at the examination. They may vary from past rubrics.
4. Read through the question paper carefully.
5. Choose the questions that you propose to answer and make brief notes. If inspiration fails, look at another question. It is better to lose a little time selecting the right questions than to put pen to paper hurriedly only to "dry up" halfway through the question.
6. Make sure you know what the examiner requires. Is he asking for a statement of law, advice, or something else?
7. Law questions fall into two types:
(a) factual
(b) problem questions.

Factual questions present few problems. It is, however, important to give the examiner the information that he requests e.g. "What were the provisions of the Employment Protection Act 1978"? is a straightforward factual question whereas "Discuss the advantages and disadvantages of Industrial Tribunals", requires facts to be marshalled for both sides of the question.

Problem questions are set to test both knowledge of the law and application of law to the facts. The approach to this type of question is to set down clearly the law involved, which may be either statutory or case law, mention any exceptions which may be relevant, then apply the law to the facts of the question.

8. Write legibly and set out your answer intelligibly. An examiner cannot spare time to decipher a badly written answer.

9. Relate cases cited, to the text of your answer. A handful of unrelated cases added at the end of an answer will not gain marks.

10. Ensure that your answers are numbered and you have inserted numbers of the questions answered in the appropriate part of the examination paper.